Published by:
LIVING TIME ® Digital
Kemp House, 152-160 City Rd
London EC1V 2NX
United Kingdom.

© Edouard d'Araille 1996, 2001.
© *LIVING TIME* ® *Films Limited.* 1996.
© *LIVING TIME* ® *Press.* 1999, 2001, 2002.
Robbe-Grillet 80th Anniversary Edition in 2002.
Reprinted in 2003 (twice), 2004, 2005, 2006,
and 2007 (three times) by *LTP* ™.

- E. d'Araille has asserted his right under
the Copyright, Designs and Patent Act 1988,
to be identified as the author of this conference.
This text is a transcription of the Proceedings
of the Oxford University Alain Robbe-Grillet
Conference 1996 '*In the Temple of Dreams*'.

All Rights Reserved. No part of this publication
may be reproduced, stored in a retrieval system,
or be transmitted in any form, or by any means -
electronic, mechanical, photocopying, recording or
otherwise - without having the previous permission
of the publisher of this work: *LIVING TIME* ® *Press.*

ISBN 978-1-903331-17-0

British Library *Cataloguing in Publication* Data.
A Bibliographic (*CIP*) Catalogue record is
available from The British Library.

Every reasonable effort has been
made to trace copyright holders of material
reproduced in this book, but if any have been
inadvertently overlooked then the publishers
would be glad to hear from them.

email: info@livingtime.co.uk
website: www.livingtime.net
telephone: 0207-1014141
rights: 07930-128892

In the Temple of Dreams
the writer on the screen

*"Je regarde,
donc je dérobe"*

ALAIN ROBBE-GRILLET

**PROCEEDINGS OF THE OXFORD UNIVERSITY
ROBBE-GRILLET CONFERENCE, SEPT. 1996**

presented by Edouard d'Araille

LIVING TIME® Press

**Dedicated to
Jérôme Lindon
(1920 – 2001)**

A PUBLISHER OF VISION
AND A MAN OF GRACE

In the Temple of Dreams
the writer on the screen

0. In the Temple of Dreams *Editor's Foreword*		Edouard d'Araille	ii
1. Alain Robbe-Grillet *Opening Words*		Prof. Ian Christie FBA	1
2. Au Temple des Rêves *L'Ecrivain à l'Ecran*		Alain Robbe-Grillet	3
3. Question-Time: *A Brief Dialogue*	with	Alain Robbe-Grillet	22
4. Magritte, Robbe-Grillet and La Belle Captive *Specular Pleasures*		Prof. Ben Stoltzfus	26
5. A Sojourn in the Maison de Rendez-Vous *Narrative Play in Robbe-Grillet*		Prof. Roch C. Smith	40
6. Text, Film et Code *Dysnarration et Cohérence*		Prof. Van den Heuvel	56
7. The Blue Villa *Within the Temple of Dreams*		Prof. Anthony Fragola	77
8. Sado-Erotic Surfaces *The 'Real' and the 'Represented' in "Nouvelles Autobiographies"*		Prof. Raylene Ramsay	93
9. The Mirror of Meta-Fiction *Robbe-Grillet as the Writerly Reader of Trans-Europ-Express*		Prof. Royal S. Brown	114
10. Open Discussion (All Participants)	*hosted by*	Ann Jefferson	129
00. Alain Robbe-Grillet *Bibliography/Filmography (All Major Works)*			148

0. In the Temple of Dreams
Editor's Foreword
Edouard d'Araille

ALTHOUGH this volume may not be in need of any Introduction - in the light of the names of the participants present at the conference it represents - let me nonetheless say just a few words about its contents, so as to make clearer the reason and circumstances of the event which it documents like a 'textual film'.

In 1996 I put myself in the position of organizing a conference which would address the relationship between, essentially, the novels and the fiction films of the writer and film-maker, Alain Robbe-Grillet. My motivation for doing so was that I was, at that time, commencing a documentary, and desired to hear from, as well as interview, numerous key authorities on Robbe-Grillet's life and work. Having attended film-viewings every week at the Maison Française while at Oxford University, I decided upon this as an ideal location for the conference. However, unlike most major conferences, which take years to plan, the 1996 ARG Conference was only arranged less than half a year in advance though the response from academics was outstanding. Over a dozen participants arrived from as far away as California and New Zealand, and the conference was attended by over fifty students and appreciators of Alain Robbe-Grillet's work. It was, in fact, a last-minute success.

EDITOR'S FOREWORD

My enthusiasm for the film-works of Alain Robbe-Grillet was so great at that time that I had organized a Retrospective of all his films at the French Institute in London, taking place in the fortnight leading up to the UK Première of his new film - *Un Bruit Qui Rend Fou* - of which I was also the distributor. All this created the perfect backdrop against which to begin an investigation into the relationship between writing and cinema, through a consideration of the work of a figure who had spent as much energy making films as he had done writing novels and short stories. How did he see the relations between these activities himself? Furthermore, aware of the dreamic qualities, both in his novels and films, I wanted Alain Robbe-Grillet and the participants to discuss this aspect of his work in particular, the degree to which his creations rest on a line that is midway between the consciousness of day and the subconscious of the night.

Both of these topics were discussed by Robbe-Grillet in depth during his talk (the first of the day), although the fields of discussion ranged far wider than these, as he related a series of pertinent observations and anecdotes relating to fiction and film. Robbe-Grillet did not read from any notes but spoke lucidly, fluently and comprehensibly in *ad lib* fashion and was the stand-out performance of the conference. I did not tell any of the participants what they should speak about on the day of the conference, though I explained to them in as much detail as possible the main thread of the conference and did my best to ensure that as varied a spectrum of ideas and themes should be represented during the day's talks.

EDITOR'S FOREWORD

Although the novels and essays of Robbe-Grillet are widely appreciated, it still remains for his film-works, of vital importance in the history of cinema, to reach the full audience for which they were intended. And though this will happen over the coming years, my only intention is that the present volume will awaken new interest in the works, both cinematic and literary, of this key figure in the movement of the 'New Novel'. Each of the separate talks provokes new debate and creates points of departure for further discussion. And even though we have moved into the Third Millennium since the conference took place, on September 25th, 1996, as I reread the words that were spoken back then I realize that they are no less relevant to literature today than they were in 1996 or at the height of the 'New Novel' movement of the 50's onwards. Nor will they be less relevant in the future.

The conference quite naturally centered on the most recent books that Robbe-Grillet had published (his *Nouvelles Autobiographies*) and the most recent film that he had directed (*Un Bruit Qui Rend Fou*). However, almost all of his other works are discussed or referred to at some point in the day's discussion. I think that everyone interested in Robbe-Grillet's work will find something stimulating in the day's talks. As for the present, Alain Robbe-Grillet's activities do not cease or abate at all. He is publishing two new texts over the coming year, and will be filming his tenth full-length feature film (his second film venture with Dimitri De Clercq). He appears, in fact, to be no less productive now than he was as a young man, an eternal battler who simply refuses to stop creating.

EDITOR'S FOREWORD

My aim, in the present text, has been to present as accurate a transcript as possible of the *1996 Alain Robbe-Grillet Oxford Conference*. My desire has not been to provide a "Critical Edition" of this work - all lectures re-written by the speakers for the new purpose, brimming with footnotes and containing a comprehensive index - rather, my desire is that you experience the flow of the conference for yourself, not changed in any substantial way whatsoever. I hope that this will stimulate new and refreshing debate.

I have not included a separate Acknowledgements in this volume, but heartfelt thanks must go to all who were involved in the events of September/October of 1996, both in Oxford and at the French Institute. Thanks to Robbe-Grillet for his key contribution to the conference, and to all of the speakers of the day. Furthermore, I must also extend my deepest gratitude to all those who made the Conference and the Retrospective possible: family and friends, crew members and colleagues, as well as all the audience and readers who attended the programme of events.

For those who are interested, a video-film of the entire conference will soon be available in a four-tape box set, including additional interviews with each of the participants and a second version of the same talk which Alain Robbe-Grillet delivered at the French Institute. Further details are contained in the full *Living Time* ® *Press* Catalogue. Details are also already available concerning the release of the new documentary **"Last Year at Marianské Lazné"** which will be screened next year to celebrate Robbe-Grillet's 80th birthday (on the 18th of August, 2002).

Special Acknowledgements

Living Time® Press would like to pay gratitude to Nomad Films for their permission to use images from their film 'The Blue Villa' on the cover, as well as within the image section in this volume (in the illustrated edition of the volume). In particular, the publisher would like to thank Dimitri and Jacques DeClercq, who have been of positive support to the Oxford Conference and the Film Retrospective from the very beginning. Their recognition of the greatness of Robbe-Grillet's film-works is what has prevented these films from being lost on the wayside, and instead, becoming part of the repertoire of cinema history.

ALDERSON SMITH, PUBLISHER

PORTRAIT DE L'AUTEUR

ALAIN ROBBE-GRILLET (1922 -   )
with Edouard d'Araille [1996].

In the Temple of Dreams

the writer on the screen

1. Alain Robbe-Grillet
Opening Words
Ian Christie FBA
Fellow of Magdalen College, Oxford
Professor of Film Studies (University of Kent)

Certainly, for someone of my generation, the work of Alain Robbe-Grillet is absolutely central to the possibility that cinema might acquire some of the complexity and modernity of literature. I still vividly remember queuing until two in the morning to see *Last Year at Marienbad* as an undergraduate in 1963 in Belfast. The film was so notorious and popular that screenings were held around the clock in a cinema near the university, and I believe people were still queuing at four o'clock in the morning. It is difficult, perhaps, to imagine people queuing today, to see a film as remarkable and experimental as *Last Year at Marienbad*. But it did happen, I was there, and I remember also the impact made by *The Immortal One* and *The Man Who Lies* when those were also shown in Britain.

Sadly, it has been increasingly difficult to see the film works of Alain Robbe-Grillet in Britain; and it says something about our draconian cinema censorship system, which has prevented some of Robbe-Grillet's work being circulated. Britain is the only country in the world which has statutory legal censorship for video, which keeps a lot of challenging and controversial work out of circulation. Unfortunately, therefore, some of his more recent work has not been seen, except in private screenings, which I think is a pity, because Robbe-Grillet has continued to make films and to push forward the boundaries of what is possible on the screen, in parallel with his literary work.

So this is a double career; that of a writer who works on the screen and on the page, and who has continued to do so for an extraordinary span of time. Robbe-Grillet's example renews the hope that film can be seen as involved in a similar enterprise to writing, a hope that is often forgotten in Britain, where cinema exists in a compartment labelled 'entertainment', and too often lacks the ambition, and complexity, that literature can aspire to.

Ian Christie

Oxford University, September 25th 1996

2. Au Temple des Rêves:
L'Ecrivain sur L'Ecran
Alain Robbe-Grillet

Ce n'est pas moi qui ai fixé le titre de mon intervention. C'est un problème qui s'est jamais posé pour moi - comment on fasse de romans et de films. Mais, c'est un problème qui, visiblement, se pose pour tout le monde. C'est une question qu'on va me poser dès le début, et qu'on continue encore à me poser toujours. *Comment est-ce qu'un romancier peut faire des films?*

Or, je ne suis pas un romancier. Je suis ingénieur de recherches agronomiques, spécialiste des maladies de bananes. Alors, tous vont me demander - *comment est-ce qu'un ingénieur de recherches agronomiques peut écrire des romans?* C'est une chose qui a nuit à ma stature de cinéaste, parce que j'avais été 'classé' comme romancier. Je ne sais pas si c'est pareil en Angleterre, mais en France c'est terrible. C'est à dire que, classé comme ça, on n'a pas le droit d'en sortir. Or, je fais de la peinture aussi, n'est-ce pas, et j'aurais fait volontiers de la musique si j'avais eu une connaissance suffisante.

Alors, je vais donc pas m'étendre sur la façon où je suis passé de la littérature au cinéma, car je ne suis pas 'passé de la littérature au cinéma'. J'ai fait des romans, et j'ai fait des films, et jamais je vais publier un roman à partir d'un de mes films, et jamais je vais

In the Temple of Dreams

faire un film à partir d'un de mes romans. C'est à dire que les producteurs sont toujours rassurés par la littérature qu'ils auraient aimé que je porte à l'écran - les romans qui ont commencé à être célèbre, comme *Le Voyeur* et *La Jalousie* - mais j'ai toujours refusé, parce que pour moi *ce sont des romans*.

C'est à dire que, si j'ai une idée de récit en tête, je sais immédiatement si c'est un roman ou c'est un film. Si ce projet en tête, ce sont des structures de phrases, des structures de langages, des structures de vocabulaire et de prosodie - je sais que c'est un roman; si j'ai en tête des images et des sons, je sais que c'est un film - et il n'y a absolument pas de moyen de passer de l'un à l'autre. C'est personnel. Vous savez que Marguerite Duras, par exemple, au contraire, a fait souvent un roman et un film avec le même projet de récit. C'est à dire que, pour elle, elle pouvait passer d'un médium à l'autre. Il faut dire aussi que les films de Marguerite Duras sont entièrement basés sur une 'parole'; c'est à dire, qu'on va mettre des images sur cette parole, images qui sont pour elle, *visiblement*, peu importantes - puisque, autant la bande sonore des films de Marguerite Duras est soignée, travaillée, parfaite, autant en les images on a l'impression que c'est 'n'importe quoi' (mais je ne dis pas ça du tout comme une critique). Une fois elle a même fait un film où c'était délibérément, demonstrativement, 'n'importe quoi'. C'est à dire qu'il y avait une caméra dans une voiture, elle était dans la voiture, et la caméra filmait en continu tous ce qu'on voyait par la fenêtre. En général on voyait rien dehors, et ça n'était pas gênant du tout, n'est-ce pas? Et il n'y a pas un montage après, c'est à dire que c'est les bobines, entières, qu'on a fait collées, l'une après l'autre. Je crois que le film s'appelle *Aurélia Steiner II*.

Pour moi, au contraire, c'est absolument impératif, les images et les sons, qu'on peut essayer de transformer en mots. Mais c'est pas comme ça [Duras] que je peux procéder. Les mots sont des mots, les images sont des images. Ce qui fait que, le seul cinéaste avec qui j'ai pu collaborer, c'est Alain Resnais, parce qu'Alain Resnais a accepté que je lui décrive un film. C'est à dire que, pour *L'Année Dernière à Marienbad*, j'allais pas écrire un récit que lui va transformer en film. J'ai décrit un film. C'est à dire que, ce qu'on *voit* et ce qu'on *entend*, je l'ai *décrit*, image par image, avec les positions de caméra et les mouvements d'appareils etc. Je ne suis pas allé au tournage, c'est Resnais qui l'a réalisé, et, par conséquent, il a tout repris en main. Mais, il a accepté que je lui donne le récit d'un film qui aurait déjà été fait, c'est à dire, un film qui était dans ma tête, et que je décrivais en tant que film. C'est extrêmement rare de la part d'un grand metteur-en-scène, comme Resnais, d'accepter une chose pareille.

À la même époque, Michelangelo Antonioni voulait faire un film avec moi. Comme j'avais beaucoup d'admiration pour l'oeuvre d'Antonioni, j'avais accepté tout de suite, et on se voyait beaucoup. Et, tant qu'on parlait en général d'un projet de film - ce que pourrait être le film - tout marchait très bien, mais quand j'ai commencé à parler de *ce film-là*, qu'on

In the Temple of Dreams

allait faire, j'ai dit: "Au début, on voit sur l'écran . . ." - il m'a arrêté tout de suite. Il m'a dit "*Ah non! Tu me racontes une histoire, et **moi** je te dis ce qu'on voit sur l'écran.*" C'est à dire que pour Antonioni - qui a pu utiliser beaucoup de scénaristes - le scénariste doit lui raconter une histoire, et lui, il fait ce qu'on appelle 'l'adaptation'. C'est à dire, il la transforme en images - cadrées, montées etc. . . Et alors je lui ai répondu: "Ecoutes, on va pas travailler ensembles, parce que, si je pense à un film, je pense pas à une histoire, je pense à ce qu'on voit, et à ce qu'on entend. Et si tu veux une histoire, tu n'as qu'à prendre un de mes romans (parce qu'il y avait déjà deux ou trois qui étaient publiés à l'époque) et les adapter au cinéma." Il y a pensé d'ailleurs, puis il y a renoncé, et donc nous n'avons plus de projets ensembles pendant de longues années. On a continué à se voir, et j'ai maintenant un nouveau projet avec Antonioni, mais c'est lui comme acteur, et moi comme cinéaste. Et donc là, c'est tout à fait autre chose!

Une question qu'on peut se poser, c'est - *Comment se fait-il qu'on m'ait proposé de faire des films?* Beaucoup de gens ont des films imaginaires en tête. Sartre voulait faire des films - on n'a jamais laissé - et il est pourtant beaucoup plus célèbre que moi. Pourquoi est-ce que des producteurs sont venus me demander si je voulais faire un film comme réalisateur? Et ça, c'est une question bizarre, où la réponse ne peut être que bizarre. Je pense que c'est par erreur! C'est un malentendu! C'est à dire, un producteur lit *La Jalousie* et se dit "*Voyons, voilà un garçon qui écrit un roman, mais qu'est ce que c'est que ce roman? C'est la description d'une maison - la terrasse, le jardin autour, le couloir, la salle à manger etc. . . . - alors, il met deux cents pages à décrire une maison, et après deux cent pages on ne sait toujours pas comment elle est faite! Alors, c'est un peu embêtant, parce qu'il n'y a pas autre chose dans le roman. On va lui donner une caméra, et il prendra sa photo et on saura enfin de quoi il parle!"*

C'est à dire que, c'est l'époque où j'étais réputé être un écrivain objectif, c'est à dire, que je décrivais les objets, mais de manière objective. Le mot 'objectif' avait été employé par Roland Barthes, et après donc a eu une 'entente' considérable. On proposait de me classer 'objectiviste', ce qui est effectivement beaucoup plus approprié. Mais alors, à la fin des années cinquantes, début des années soixantes, j'étais censé faire une littérature qui enregistrait le monde tel qu'il était, comme reflète une caméra. On parlait de '*L'Ecole du Regard*'. Et donc, des producteurs me demandent faire un film. Ces producteurs étaient des producteurs qui venaient de produire *Hiroshima Mon Amour*. C'est à dire, des producteurs audacieux qui s'engageaient à Paris sur des choses que la profession trouvait bizarre.

Vous savez que Resnais était à l'époque un réalisateur de courts-métrages, et la profession avait décidé que Resnais ne pourrait faire *que* des courts-métrages, parce que là aussi, n'est-ce pas, il y avait la 'classification'. "*Si on fait de courts-métrages, on ne peut pas faire de longs-métrages. C'est pas la même chose, pas le même travail.*" Donc Resnais avait été classé 'courts-métrages', mais un producteur qui

In the Temple of Dreams

pensait que Resnais était un réalisateur de longs-métrages, décide de faire faire un long-métrage. Monté comme souvent sur une combinaison plus ou moins louche, les japonais avaient cherché un réalisateur pour faire un film sur la bombe atomique. Et Resnais, qui avait fait les documentaires sur les grandes questions de l'époque - les camps de concentration, des choses comme ça, n'est-ce pas - semblait à tout indiquer approprié pour cet autre catastrophe mondial. Et donc, il pose la question à Resnais - "*Est-ce que vous voulez faire un film sur la bombe atomique?*" Il dit "Mais oui, pourquoi pas? Mais il faut que le scénario soit écrit par une femme." C'était la seule chose que demandait Resnais. Et donc à ce moment des hésitations ont eu lieu entre Simone de Beauvoir, Françoise Sagan et Marguerite Duras. Marguerite Duras a accepté tout de suite et a 'évacué' Hiroshima et la bombe atomique immédiatement en quelques phrases dès le début du film: "**Non. Non. Tu n'as rien vu à Hiroshima.**" Et elle raconte la seule histoire de la personne qui court dans tout son oeuvre. C'est l'histoire d'une jeune française qui couche avec un soldat allemand pendant l'occupation allemande en France.

Et, évidemment, le film a eu un très grand succès - d'abord 'estime', puis de public - dans tout les pays du monde, sauf le Japon! On a trouvé que ce drame n'est même pas japonais, que l'histoire de *Hiroshima* a été traité 'un peu dessous la jambe'. Mais les producteurs ont réussi leur coup, et, l'année suivante, ils décident qu'ils vont me faire faire un film. Et, là aussi, ils viennent me demander "*Est-ce que vous voulez réaliser un film?*" "Vous savez déjà mes romans, et le public qui existe n'est pas celui du Rex, des grandes salles de cinémas de Paris." "Ça va, ça n'a aucune importance. La seule chose c'est qu'il faut tourner en Turquie." Alors je dis "Pourquoi en Turquie?" "*Bien, c'est parce que les affaires sont comme ça.*"

Un marchand de laine belge avait des fonds importants bloqués en Turquie. Or, la livre turque n'était pas exportable. C'était une monnaie qu'on pouvait dépenser en Turquie mais qu'on ne pouvait exporter aux autres pays du monde. Et, le producteur Samy Halfon s'en va proposer à ce marchand de laine une solution ingénieuse. On va dépenser cet argent turque pour faire un film. La livre turque n'est exportable, mais le film, oui, il est. Le film sortira en France. Il gagnera de fortune en France, et l'argent sera récupéré par le marchand de laine. Alors, tout est bien marché, sauf que le film n'a pas eu un grand succès du tout, bien qu'il a eu le *Prix Louis Delluc,* qui est la plus prestigieuse de récompenses pour un jeune réalisateur. Le film a eu vraiment très peu de succès, parce que ce n'était pas comme ça qu'on devait faire un film, parait-il.

Donc, je parle d'Istamboul. Il se trouvait que par hasard le producteur m'a demandé - "*Vous voulez tourner ceci à Turquie?*" J'ai dit, "Mais oui, très content." Et pourquoi? Parce qu'il se trouvait que tout à fait par hasard c'est à Istamboul que dix ans auparavant j'avais fait la connaissance d'une petite fille qui est devenue ma femme. Et donc j'étais lié, sentimentalement, à cette ville d'Istamboul, et tourner une

In the Temple of Dreams

histoire d'amour à Istamboul avec Samy Halfon me semblait tout à fait une chose intéressante. Donc, je m'installe à Istamboul avec Catherine et je commence à écrire un découpage, directement, un découpage en décor naturel, avec pour chaque plan, la position de la caméra marquée avec un signe que je retrouverais plus tard. C'est-à-dire que c'était complètement conçu comme un film.

Et puis, ce travail est interrompu.

Alors, le producteur, évidemment, avait négocié avec les autorités turques, et les autorités turques avait trouvé le projet de l'histoire un peu bizarre. Ils avaient dit, "*Bon, ça ira, mais il faudra qu'on voie la foule acclamant Menderes.*" Et alors, moi qui comptait montrer un Istamboul complètement vide, silencieux etc. - il y avait tout d'un coup un plan de foules acclamant Menderes. C'était formidable! Alors, j'acceptais tout de suite! Et, malheureusement, il y a la révolution sanglante, et Menderes est pendu. Le père de notre actrice turque, qui était le ministre de l'intérieur, est pendu aussi. Ça va très mal. Je rentre à Paris, et à ce moment-là un producteur, un autre producteur, me demande si je veux écrire le deuxième film de Resnais.

Donc, après *Hiroshima Mon Amour*, ça devait être le deuxième film de Resnais. J'avais beaucoup d'admiration pour les courts-métrages de Resnais, et pour *Hiroshima Mon Amour*. Je dis **oui** immédiatement. Resnais continuait à hésiter entre Françoise Sagan et Simone de Beauvoir. Évidemment, c'est pas tout à fait la même chose. C'était pas une idée de Resnais là, de s'adresser à moi, c'était une idée du producteur. On m'a dit "*Ecrivez trois projets*", et pendant une nuit j'ai écrit trois 'synopsis', c'est à dire, trois fois deux pages. Il donne ça à Resnais, qui dit "*C'est formidable. Je peux les tourner, tous les trois.*" Mais il va falloir en choisir *une,* parce qu'on voudra que j'en écrive *une.*

Je n'avais pas encore compris à ce moment-là que ce qu'il cherchait, c'était un film pour Delphine Seyrig. Il venait d'enlever Delphine Seyrig à son mari légitime, qui était un bon peintre américain, Jack Hugermann (il y a un très bon tableau au *Musée de Faleau* qui s'appelle '*Delphine*', un tableau de Hugermann. Tous les gens pensent que c'est 'Dauphin', parce qu'ils ne savent pas qu'il était le mari légitime de Delphine Seyrig). Et donc Resnais cherchait un film pour Delphine Seyrig. Et, tout d'un coup alors il se dit que ces trois projets, et en particulier le projet de *L'Année Dernière à Marienbad,* lui convenaient parfaitement.

J'écris le film comme un découpage, c'est à dire, plan par plan, et Resnais n'a discuté absolument rien. Il se comportait de découper mon texte pour le mettre sur deux colonnes, parce que c'était le temps où on mettait encore le cinéma sur deux colonnes, colonne *images*, colonne *sons*. Alors, il découpait mon manuscrit pour le repartir sur des pages droites et des pages gauches. Et ensuite, pendant le tournage . . [Robbe-Grillet suddenly returns to talking about *l'Immortelle*] . . alors moi j'étais pas au tournage car j'ai écrit ça en deux mois et puis la situation en Turquie s'était normalisé, et j'étais retourné là-bas. J'avais continué le projet. J'avais demandé seulement: "Qu'est-ce que je fais du plan où la foule acclame Menderes, parce qu'il a été pendu?" Cependant, ils n'aimaient pas tellement ce genre de plaisanterie. C'est drôle, le tournage de *l'Immortelle*, parce que, comme c'était un film officiellement turque, il y avait un représentant du ministère de l'intérieur qui était là au tournage, et a assisté à tous les plans, etc. Il commençait par contester le choix des figurants. J'avais demandé, par exemple, que les ouvriers passent dans la rue, qui convoquent des figurants, qui sont tous habillés en costumes croisés et cravates etc., et le ministre m'a dit "*Vous avez bonne impression de la Turquie, hein!?*" Et puis alors ensuite il regardait les gens tels qu'ils étaient placés, pour voir si ça allait donner une bonne image de la Turquie, ce qui est vraiment très bien. Il n'avait pas compris que l'objectif qu'on mettait dans la caméra changeait tout. On était au premier plan des gens vachement bien habillés, et on ne les verrait pas sur l'écran, puisque la caméra passait en haut et filmait tous les gens qui avaient des 'Têtes de Turques', comme on dirait en français.

Pendant que Resnais tournait *L'Année Dernière à Marienbad* à München, pendant cette heure-là, je continuais à écrire *l'Immortelle*. C'est bien discuté si *L'Année Dernière à Marienbad* ou *l'Immortelle* est antérieur à l'autre. Il est certain que *L'Année Dernière à Marienbad* est défini avant, mais il a été commencé après. Ils sont contemporains, bien que tout à fait différents, car quand j'ai écrit *L'Année dernière à Marienbad* c'était pour Resnais. C'est à dire que le cinéma de Resnais que j'aimais n'était pas forcément le cinéma que j'avais envie de faire. En particulier, il y a, dans *L'Année Dernière à Marienbad*, de très longues '*travellings*' au début, et dans tout le film, qui sont extrêmement important pour le récit. Ces '*travellings*' n'ont pas été rajoutés par Resnais. C'est moi qui les décris, mais je les ai décrit en tant que '*travellings*' de Resnais, c'est à dire que l'oeuvre de Resnais que je connaissais était déjà en somme incorporé dans notre propre projet. Et je décris jamais de '*travellings'* pour mes propres films, parce que d'abord ça coûte trop cher, et, parce que j'aime les plans fixes. J'aime tourner les plans fixes, ce qui ne veut pas dire que je n'aime pas les '*travellings'* de Resnais.

Voilà donc comment c'est passé le passage de l'un à l'autre, mais j'ai continué à écrire des romans. Et là maintenant alors, comme je ne fais un roman, un film, un roman, un film, un roman, un film, comme je fais quelquefois deux films, coup sur coup, que j'ai fait trois romans coup sur coup, quand j'ai fait deux films on me dit alors "*Monsieur Robbe-Grillet, on a abandonné la littérature?*" - Je dis "Non, non. Mais je ne peux pas tout faire à la fois. Vous savez, je travaille lentement." Et quand j'écris un roman on me dit "*Le cinéma, c'est fini?*" "Non. Je fais des romans et des films, mais dans l'ensemble je suis peu productif." John Ford a fait une masse de films - à peu pres soixante longs-métrages, je crois!

Alors, je vais parler maintenant très brièvement d'un point qui m'importe sur les différences que je ressens pendant le travail. C'est à dire qu'il y a quelque chose pour moi - d'une part sur les images et les sons à côté, et les mots de l'autre - quelque chose qui sépare ces deux domaines de façon presque encore plus radical. C'est que *le roman est un travail solitaire; le cinéma est un travail de groupe.*

Le dernier film que j'ai fait, *Un Bruit Qui Rend Fou*, a été co-réalisé avec un de mes étudiants de *l'Ecole de Cinéma de New York*, Dimitri De Clercq. Et, tout le monde me demandent - "*Mais comment est-ce qu'on peut co-réaliser un film?*" Je dis, "Ecoutez. Expliquez-moi comment pourrait-on faire un film tout seul?" Si, il y a un cinéaste belge qui s'appelle Boris Lehmann, qui est très célèbre dans les salles belges. Lui, il fait *tout* alors. Il est le propre producteur, l'acteur, le scénariste, le chef-opérateur, le machiniste etc. . . Mais ça n'est pas possible dans le 'cinéma normal', c'est à dire, normalement produit.

Il y a forcément des gens. Il y a des gens qui sont *là*. En particulier, les acteurs et les techniciens. Et puis il y a *le monde* qui est là. Si je suis à ma table et j'écris "Il pleut à courants", j'ai pas besoin attendre un jour de pluie pour écrire ça. Je peux écrire ça, et ça ne coûte rien à personne, et le lecteur qui ouvrira mon livre et qui lira "Il pleut à courants" n'a pas regardé dehors pour voir que je suis un menteur! J'aime bien voire me servir du monde solide tel qu'il est - la vraie ville d'Istamboul. Quand Resnais avait proposé de tourner *L'Année Dernière à Marienbad* devant des toiles peintes - parce que ça coûte moins cher - j'ai répondu tout de suite "Ah non, c'est une histoire de phantômes. Des phantômes devant des toiles peintes - ça n'existe pas! Les phantômes ont quelque chose de solide, quelque chose de réel."

Et c'est vrai que j'accorde une très grosse importance au monde réel tel qu'il est. Je vais le transformer ensuite par l'allitération, par des prises de vue, et coup sur coup par le montage; mais ce monde solide, il faut que j'en tienne compte.

Et ça je pensais déjà au moment de *l'Immortelle*, mais à ce moment-là je pensais que les acteurs pouvaient être contraints. C'est à dire, j'avais déjà éprouvé des difficultés dans le choix des acteurs. Les acteurs, les personnages d'un roman, n'ont pas besoin de ressembler à quelqu'un qui existe vraiment. Au cinéma, il va falloir trouver quelqu'un qui existe, et qui va incarner cet acteur. Et à partir du moment où ce quelqu'un était choisi, il va avoir un rôle créateur dans le film, que le public sait très bien. Le public va voir un film d'Alain Delon en ignorant complètement le nom du réalisateur. Et, je me suis aperçu pendant le tournage de *l'Immortelle* qu'il fallait non pas chercher des acteurs pour l'histoire que j'avais écrit, mais écrire des histoires pour des acteurs avec qui on avait envie de travailler. Les deux films que j'ai fait ensuite - *Trans-Europ-Express* et *L'Homme Qui Ment* (et *l'Immortelle* aussi) - sont des films qui avaient étés écrits pour Trintignant, c'est à dire, en fonction justement, parce que j'étais chez Trintignant. Et donc, il ne s'agit pas de les [the actors] contraindre, mais au contraire de les laisser faire avec des choses. Le travail avec Trintignant, par exemple, consiste à lui faire tourner un truc que j'ai vu dans ma tête. Et puis, après de nombreuses reprises qui ne sont jamais des doubles, qui sont toujours des variantes - c'est à dire, les prises ont été fait un peu autre chose - je me sers au montage de l'ensemble des prises. C'est pas du tout *une* que j'ai choisi. Et bien, ensuite, après la dernière prise qui est faite par Trintignant, je lui dis "Qu'est-ce que tu as envie de faire dans cette scène-là?" Il le fait. Et là aussi je peux m'en servir, ou non pas m'en servir, ou m'en servir partiellement. En littérature, je ne peux pas. Même Henri de Corinthe, qui est pourtant sympathique, je peux pas lui dire, tout d'un coup, "*Tiens, tu vas jouer la scène tout seul, moi je suis fatigué.*" Il faut absolument là, que la présence dans mon texte littéraire est totale.

Bon, évidemment je respecte la langue française. Le vocabulaire et la grammaire sont respectés. Ça, c'est une contrainte de base, mais, c'est en somme le 'code de l'expression'. Et, c'est la seule enfin. Flaubert lisait des morceaux de manuscrits à Du Camp et à Bouilhet. Leur intervention était assez malheureuse en général, et Flaubert n'écoutait pas leurs conseils. Non. J'écris seul. Même à ma femme je ne lis pas de morceaux pour en savoir ce qu'elle pense, et ce que je dois faire après. Là aussi il y a d'autres objections. Je connaissais une femme romancière soviétique qui n'a pas laissé de nom dans la littérature; qui était une brave dame, qui me disait - "*Il faut tenir compte du public.*" J'ai dit - "Ah, vous le connaissez?" Elle me dit - "*Je ne connais pas au moment où j'écris la première version, mais quand elle est publiée je reçois des lettres et je modifie la seconde version en fonction de ce que le public en pense.*" Evidemment, c'est pas économe!

Je tiens, alors, essentiellement, en tout cas personellement, à ce que le roman soit un travail solitaire. Alors que je tiens de plus en plus à ce que le film soit un travail collectif; à tel point que, après avoir écrit un vague sujet pour *Un Bruit Qui Rend Fou*, qui s'appelait d'ailleurs d'abord *Le Retour de Franck*, le film a beaucoup erré ensuite. On a fait une adaptation pour Macao, une autre pour le Vietnam, une autre pour le Cambodge, et enfin on l'a tourné en Grèce. Et, à chaque fois alors, tout ces voyages et ces adaptations, ces repérages, étaient faits en collaboration avec ce jeune homme qui avait eté mon étudiant, le seul étudiant de cinéma que j'avais eu qui eut vraiment d'imagination cinématographique. Et, peu à peu, je me suis dit "*Mais il est co-adaptateur*". C'est à dire qu'il n'est pas co-scénariste (parce que le scénario, je l'ai écrit), mais co-adaptateur, parce qu'il a pris part à faire ce qu'on appelle '*l'adaptation*' - c'est à dire, vraiment le film tel qu'on le présente. Et ensuite il est devenu vraiment co-réalisateur, car à partir du moment qu'on a tourné en Grèce et pas en Cambodge, où la dernière adaptation a été écrite, évidemment je vais le laisser prendre en main tout ce projet qu'il avait de conserver l'Asie dans une île grècque. Et, comme c'est un film phantôme en fois de plus, c'est une Asie phantôme qui est là dans cet île grècque - et par conséquent le rôle de Dimitri De Clercq est extrêmement important dans ce film. Néanmoins, c'est un film de moi, si on veut. Mais je n'ai fait, je crois, que reconnaître sur le générique, ce que beaucoup de réalisateurs vieillissants ont reconnus, mais quittant la vérité. Le dernier film d'Ozu, le dernier film de Visconti, ont été faits par leurs premiers assistants. Seulement, comme cet assistant est méconnu, et le nom du réalisateur est important pour la compagnie, il n'est pas question de dire que ce n'est pas Visconti qui l'a entièrement réalisé. Et alors, donc, le cinéma est un travail pour nous.

D'autre part, et ce sera mon dernier remarque, je voudrais justifier le fait de continuer à me servir de deux matériaux aussi différents que le texte et l'image, à me justifier pour des raisons psychiques, et même psychanalytiques.

Vous savez que les gens commencent à confondre les descriptions et les images. Il y a une confusion dans la tête du spectateur entre la description d'une chose et l'image de cette chose. C'est une confusion qui me surprend car on la retrouve souvent sous la plume d'universitaire. Une dame professeur à l'Université de Fukuoka au Japon, une dame qui est spécialiste de Flaubert, a dit une fois en classe, que si Flaubert avait vécu à l'époque du cinéma, qu'il n'aurait pas écrit de romans, qu'il aurait fait des films! On sentait très bien dans son texte que la description n'était que la reproduction d'images qu'il aurait préféré filmer directement. C'est monstrueux! C'est monstrueux parce que Flaubert a de son vivant protesté contre cette interprétation posthume de son oeuvre. Un éditeur, après le procès de *Madame Bovary*, a voulu faire de belles éditions illustrées de *Madame Bovary,* et Flaubert a refusé avec un montre de colère considérable, et il écrit une lettre à Louise Colet, pour lui dire - "*Pourquoi est-ce que je laisserais le premier imbécile venu montrer ce que j'ai eu tant de mal à cacher?!*" Donc, la notion est extrêmement moderne, et trés récent. *L'image montre, la description cache.* Il y a quelque chose dans la description qui n'est pas de l'ordre de la 'monstration', qui est de l'ordre 'dérobage'. C'est à dire, il y a quelque chose dans la description moderne - je relie plus sur Flaubert que sur Balzac - qui 'gomme' l'image, qui la fait disparaître. *Quel est le grand penseur qui a confondu l'image et le texte?*

C'est Freud. Sigmund Freud, de ce point de vue-là, a fait une erreur. Sur autres points psychiques, comment pensait Freud? Il se dit - "*Je vais explorer l'inconscient, donc, qu'est-ce qui traduit l'inconscient en un nombre de choses? - les erreurs, l'absurde, mais avant tout les rêves.*" **Les rêves**, et il se dit - "*Donc, je vais faire raconter des rêves.*" C'est ahurissant ça! Je sais pas si vous avez essayé de raconter un rêve. On s'aperçoit immédiatement que c'est impossible à raconter un rêve. Mais, Freud procède comme ça. Il demande à son patient de raconter un rêve. A ce moment-là, c'est un récit oral, c'est à dire que le récit est une approximation où le patient essaie d'exprimer son rêve. Il dit "J'ai vu ceci, et puis après", etc. C'est à dire que le texte oral n'est pas clos. Il est constamment ouvert sur des interrogations, sur les 'peut-êtres', sur les incertitudes, sur les glissements; sur même ce qui l'appelait Freud lui-même, la *condensation* et le *déplacement*, qui sont deux opérations importantes qui luisent à la descriptabilité de l'image. Mais, ça s'aggrave ensuite, car Freud écrit ce texte. Ce n'est pas le patient qui l'écrit, c'est Freud! *Il écrit*, c'est à dire, on a un texte à ce

In the Temple of Dreams

moment-là, un vrai texte écrit, qui transforme le texte oral et qui est *clos*. C'est à dire, à ce moment-là les choses sont comme ça. C'est le texte avec des mots. Les mots sont d'ailleurs les mots de Freud, puisque même il parle pas la même langue que le texte du patient. Et Freud va travailler, pendant toute son analyse, sur le texte qu'il a écrit lui-même. C'est à dire qu'une double transformation a lieu - *d'une part* on a raconté un rêve lorsqu'il est impossible, et *d'autre part* on a transcrit une parole, ce qui est également impossible. Et Freud va alors très loin, car il n'y a plus que le texte qui compte. Il voit des associations intéressantes qui sont pas dans l'allemand, mais qui sont dans une autre langue, en italien, par exemple, sans ce soucier du fait que le patient n'était pas italien. Mais comme Freud pouvait parler quelques nombres de langues, il faisait un petit peu des jeux de mots, par exemple, entre deux langues, sans se soucier de savoir que le patient ne parlait pas ces langues. C'est *son* inconscient!

Les psychanalystes modernes se sont rendus comptes très vite qu'il y avait là un problème. Et il y a une phrase de Lacan qui est assez célèbre, qu'il est justifié de travailler sur le texte écrit, car *"l'inconscient est structuré comme langue, et même on sait pas comment un texte est une langue ou la langue. Ou bien le psychanalyse est impossible"*, dit le texte de Lacan. La seconde partie de la phrase a disparu entièrement de la *doxa*, et elle est devenu un peu travaillé sur le récit du rêve car l'inconscient est structuré comme la langue. Or, qui a trouvé ça? Personne. C'est un axiom. Simplement, Lacan avait dit que systèmes comme ça étaient pas praticals. Alors, si on s'intéresse à cette espace dans la tête de l'être humain, nous avons aujourd'hui deux façons de faire des récits, deux façons à faire qui ne s'appuient pas sur le même idiom. C'est à dire, je peux faire un récit en mots. Si j'ai fait un rêve, je peux produire un récit à partir de ce rêve. Le début d'un récit est un récit de rêve. C'est à dire que j'ai mis en mots un rêve récurrent que j'ai fait toute mon enfance, une fois de plus au bord de la mer et c'est une chose qu'on peut faire. Toute la dispersion. On peut se dire aussi, "tiens, je vais essayer d'en faire un film de ce rêve", et à ce moment-là je n'ai plus besoin de passer par les mots.

Donc, la justification du roman et du film va enrichir, probablement, la connaissance problématique de la *psyché*, puisqu'il y a des choses de la technique cinématographique, qui ne sont pas transmissibles dans la langue, et il y a des choses de la langue qui ne sont pas transmissibles au cinéma. Par exemple, toute la grammaire et en particulier la conjugaison des temps qui jouent un tel rôle dans le texte. C'est une chose qui n'existe pas au cinéma, car les images sont toujours au présent. Donc chaque domaine va avoir à organiser un matériau précis, et c'est cette organisation qui va créer des formes spécifiques - formes spécifiques à la littérature et formes spécifiques au cinéma. Et ce sont ces formes qui pourraient être considérées aussi réelle (du point de vue non pas du réaliste, mais du réel), comme des *approches possibles* ou en tout cas *des chemins possibles à l'intérieur de la psyché*.

3. The Writer on the Screen

A Brief Dialogue with Alain Robbe-Grillet

Tony Fragola: You've indicated all the differences between film and written text. But there seems to me some basic principle that you were trying to deal with in both mediums. That is, the use of space, time, also the concept of the interior self - so that in both your films and your literary texts, you're trying to create the interior of a man, the imaginary world of a man, but in two different mediums. But there do seem to be basic principles that are similar in both, or that are linked to both your texts and your films.

ARG: L'espace et le temps sont justement de ces éléments problématiques du rêve, et il y a dans le rêve, par exemple, ce qu'on appelle les '*espaces paradoxaux*' - c'est à dire, un intérieur tout d'un coup est un extérieur si on avait affaire à la topologie de Klein. Et ces problèmes de l'espace, ils existent dans mon esprit très, très certainement. Il est certain qu'il va y avoir des refléts dans la littérature comme dans la langue. De la même façon, les thèmes personnels sont récurrents dans mes deux branches de récits - donc le sado-érotisme, par exemple - mais c'est justement là que ça devient intéressant pour moi, de prendre quelque chose comme mes rapports avec l'espace comme élément de construction d'un récit ou d'un film. Mais ça n'a jamais été transposé de l'un à l'autre.

Roch Smith: On parlait des différences entre les deux, et vous avez insisté sur les différences entre la langue et le film, les temps des verbes, par exemple. Mais est-ce qu'il ne s'agit jamais des temps de verbes sur l'écran, parce que les personnages parlent? C'est très fréquent, par exemple, dans *Un Bruit Qui Rend Fou*, qu'on emploie le conditionnel pour quelque chose de possible.

ARG: C'est à dire que dans le film, le film est un matériau qui est déjà polyvalent. C'est à dire que dans le film il y a du texte et les dialogues, encore plus. Et par conséquent cette partie-là, qui n'est de l'image, elle peut jouer sur les spécificités du texte à ce moment-là. Et il est tout à fait normal d'en amuser aussi. Je veux pas du tout réduire le cinéma à tout ce qui n'existe pas dans un autre art. Il y a des choses qui existent dans la nature, et des choses qui existent dans la littérature, et des choses qui existent dans la musique, puisque je me sers beaucoup de la musique dans le film. C'est d'ailleurs alors, une des choses qui aussi va opposer la littérature au cinéma - j'ai parlé de la solitude et au contraire de la collectivisation du texte cinématographique. C'est autre chose alors qui va séparer mes deux modes de récits, qui est extrêmement importante, car dans le roman tout est langue, *tout est langue*. A part mes picto-romans (le livre que j'ai fait avec Magritte, par exemple, ou avec Rauschenberg, où les images et le texte ont joués séparément et ensembles, et l'un avec l'autre, et l'un avec l'autre etc.) dans un roman au sens normal du mot, tout devient langue. S'il y a de la musique, ça va être la '*Sonate de Walter*' écrit par Proust. Il a même voulu en mettre une portée avec quelques notes pour en faire le thème - ça se fait pas! Tout dans la littérature devient la langue, alors que dans le cinéma, non. S'il y a de parole prononcée, comme parole, il peut même y avoir de texte écrit, du texte écrit sur l'écran, et de la musique, et de la peinture etc. . . Et ça c'est aussi quelque chose qui permet des investigations nouvelles, même si les romans ne sont pas des constructions spatio-temporelles comme mes propres romans. Tandis que dans le film je vais pouvoir profiter de ce que demandait déjà Eisenstein en 1927, c'est à dire, opposer ce qu'on entend à ce qu'on voit. Dans *L'Année Dernière à Marienbad* l'homme prononce la phrase - "*alors vous vous êtes dirigée vers le lit*" et sur l'écran on voit Delphine Seyrig qui avance vers la porte, c'est à dire que sur l'image elle s'enfuit, et dans la voix de l'homme elle accepte au contraire, et elle se dirige vers la lit avec tout ce que le mot comporte.

Ben Stoltzfus: Dans vos derniers romans et vos derniers films, les femmes jouent un rôle très important, et le lecteur se fait une image de la femme qui subit certaines violences, et dans les films il existent aussi ce même passage.

ARG: Mais j'ai signalé! Et ça fait pas du tout le même effet. J'ai remarqué que la violence sexuelle en question a été beaucoup plus choquant pour le spectateur dans les films que dans les romans. C'est à dire que dans les romans le texte c'est très 'Clean'. Bon, dans le film ça reste quand même, mais c'est pas de la pornographie, c'est le *Musée du Louvre*, n'est-ce pas, comme propreté de l'image. Mais néanmoins, j'ai été extraordinairement surpris de voir que dans un film comme *Glissements Progressifs Du Plaisir* - qui a été fait inspiré par *La Sorcière* de Michelet, c'est à dire à la gloire de *La Sorcière* - de voir que les deux minutes treize secondes où il y a des violences ont été retenus de vue. Mais l'image (par rapport à pouvoir d'aggression sur le spectateur) est beaucoup plus fort que le texte. Et là aussi alors ça fait une différence qui est énorme.

4. Magritte, Robbe-Grillet, and "La Belle Captive"

Specular Pleasures

Ben Stoltzfus, Professor Emeritus (University of California, Riverside)

Alain Robbe-Grillet illustrated his 1975 novel, *La Belle Captive* [The Beautiful Captive], with 77 René Magritte pictures in color and in black and white. The title derives from six Magritte paintings also entitled *La Belle Captive*, two of which were painted in 1947 and 1967. Magritte died in 1967 and had no knowledge of the writer's project, but there is every reason to believe that he would have approved of it. A sequel to Robbe-Grillet's novel was the 1983 film, also entitled *La Belle Captive*. Although not as dialogic as the novel, the film, like the novel, incorporates Magritte's art.

In the novel, Magritte's pictures do not, in the literal sense, correspond to Robbe-Grillet's written narrative. They are used, instead, as pulsive forces, as generative themes for an imaginary discourse that parallels the paintings, glosses over them, and contradicts them. Magritte's images and titles are pretexts for the novel, a text that simultaneously comments on Magritte's art while parading Robbe-Grillet's favourite themes. The mysterious, poetic and ludic structures of Magritte's art encourage a form of literary production, not only on Robbe-Grillet's part, whose narrative voice is splintered and dispersed throughout the text, but also for the audience, which produces meaning from the pictorial arrangements that illumine in oblique ways the cultural myths with which Robbe-Grillet is playing and the pleasure he derives from this creative parody.

On the novel's immediate and superficial level the "beautiful captive" is a young girl who is abducted, raped with a baluster and drowned - a reference, says the narrator, to the well-known episode of "the difficult crossing." *The Difficult Crossing* (1926) is the title of Magritte's painting depicting the picture (or is it perhaps a window?) of a storm-tossed ship being watched from inside a room by a baluster with a human eye (*BC 22* *). This initial treatment of the drowned heroine is in keeping with Robbe-Grillet's belief that woman plays a dual role in the public's mind: on the one hand she is the exalted figure of the virgin, and on the other, she is the debased figure of the victim. *La Belle Captive* dramatizes the mythology of art and woman, even as Robbe-Grillet's text stages an imaginary dialogue with Magritte's pictures. The pictures activate the novel's diegesis, whose episodes unfold without rhyme or reason. They certainly have no logic in the classic narrative sense, and the reader who reads by the old standards is disoriented, bored and disturbed by a text that seems to go nowhere and whose leaps in time and space contradict all the "laws" of good narration. Outwardly, the book is as incongruous as Magritte's

---

* These figures refer to the images in ARG's *La Belle Captive*

paintings. But it has an inner coherence, a secret thread of meaning that is thematic rather than chronological. A whole emerges that accounts for the contradictions, the gaps, and the repetitions. What we get is a synchronism comparable to a retrospective of Magritte's works that allows for themes, connections and meanings to emerge from the inchoate nature of the subject matter.

La Belle Captive, like Samuel Beckett's *The Unnameable*, has no discernible plot, few nameable characters, no particular setting, no clockable time. All it has is a shifting voice speaking in the continuous present. Eventually this voice becomes conscious of itself ("*What am I saying? And to whom?*"). The text has an awakened identity like the awakening of the narrator before relapsing into his drugged sleep (*The Cape of Storms* [1945], *BC 97*). In elaborating self-conscious discourses, both Beckett and Robbe-Grillet have been accused of killing the novel. However, as Bruce Kawin points out, in *The Mind of the Novel*, neither is obscuring the function of literature nor spinning death dirges (*280*). Both writers are awakening language from a drugged sleep, infusing it with new potential. This art talks about itself so that it can be itself. The parameters of its self-consciousness mime the parameters of the audience's world by stressing the function of language art as a system within the limits of consciousness.

Magritte's and Robbe-Grillet's art also subvert some of the West's controlling fantasy system. They do so not by destroying art, but by turning its processes back on themselves, i.e. by parodying society's structures and mythology. In her book, *Fantasy, the Literature of Subversion*, Rosemary Jackson argues that fantasy, in and of itself, is subversive because it provides alternative ways of imagining the structures of society and the ideology of the establishment. Insofar as fantasy appeals to the unconscious - to the feelings that society represses - Jackson concludes that the formal and thematic features of fantastic art are determined by our attempt to find a language for desire (62). If Freud is right, fantasies express libidinal drives "*toward pleasure*", the libido being that part of the self that wrestles with the reality principle. The libido, insomuch as it is the locus of desire, and with pleasure as its goal, constantly strives to overcome the restraints of reality. In reflexive art, it is the restraints of realism that are constantly being challenged. Such art is subversive because it has different pleasures in mind than the ones sanctioned by society.

Because western cultures place such heavy emphasis on buying, Magritte's and Robbe-Grillet's art underscore not the consumption of a text, but the production of one. The goal of a literary work, says Roland Barthes in S/Z, is to make the reader a producer of the text, not a consumer (4). Robbe-Grillet illustrates the production of meaning - one of the sources of the "*pleasure of the text*" - with Magritte's *The Master of the Revels* (1928) (*Le maître du plaisir, BC 123*), a painting that is worth describing in some detail. In the foreground, inside a room, is a baluster, like the one used to deflower Vanessa and to wound her brother, David (*BC 23*). The baluster

In the Temple of Dreams

inside is connected by a tightrope to the smokestack of a factory outside, situated at the water's edge. But the "*reality*" of the factory is suspect: is it seen through a window, is it a painting on the wall of the room, or is it no more than a reflection in a mirror? The smokestack is as nebulous as the creature evolving on the tightrope. This "*master*" is none other than Magritte's bell (the "*grelot*") that has grown legs and a head - an image that transcends the wound of *Memory* (1942). Moreover, this living object is now on fire - a flaming performance that is dramatized further by a set of curtains framing the room.

In *Pour une Theorie du Nouveau Roman* Ricardou notes that "*flaming fiction*" ("*fiction flamboyante*", as he calls it) defines the "*Nouveau Roman*": it "*illumines*" the product and "*consumes*" itself in the process. It "*enlightens*" the reader even as it self-destructs (see *The Fanatics* [1945], *BC 33*). "*Condemned repeatedly to rise again, another, from its own ashes, it resembles the contradictory wearer of feathers that Mallarmé, by hypogram, takes pleasure in dislocating: fea-nix, Phoenix*" (219). The English translation cannot render the full range of verbal play. "*Fire-naught*" and Phoenix (in English) are too far apart for effective paronomasia. I have tried to approximate the French sound (*feu-nixe, le phénix*) though not the meaning, by playing on the word "feathers", hence the spelling "f-e-a" for "fea-nix". Fire is the origin of this delightful ambiguity of language, and if fire connotes pleasure and sexuality, then *The Master of the Revels* becomes the code-image of the artist walking the tightrope between the creative act, the production of meaning, and consumption as a pleasurable activity. Viewed from a certain angle, Magritte's painting becomes an image of reified desire.

Beneath the reveler's tightrope several steps connect the room inside with the factory outside. Both Freud and Jacques Derrida stress the sexual symbolism of steps. Says Derrida in *La Vérité en Peinture*: "*Ever since Jacob, each time we dream of a sexual act, it represents symbolically an ascent or a rapid descent.*" And says Freud (in *Traumdeutung*): "*Stairs, ladders, a step or the rung on a ladder, going up as well as down, are symbolic representations of the sexual act*" (*193*). The steps in *The Master of the Revels* (1928) resemble the steps in *The Difficult Crossing* (1926) and in *The Birth of the Idol* (1926). There is also *The Ladder of Fire* (1939) whose title provides the rungs for the symbolic ascent Derrida refers to. In *The Master of the Revels*, production, consumption and desire all contribute to the master's pleasurable performance. He is on fire.

Fire burns holes in the text, opens it up, invites audience collaboration. The reader/viewer has to perform his/her own balancing act, and, following the artist's example, s/he stages or reassembles objects, people, names, and places in unusual and unconventional ways. This is the "*bricolage*" so frequently referred to by the practitioners of the "*Nouveau Roman*". In addition to assembling objects, they take snippets of myth and exaggerate them. They play with *doxas*, exposing their arbitrariness. They create works that are deliberately anti-natural in order to emphasize the man-made. The artist's deviance is thus a departure from and even a flaunting of the so-called natural codes, because, as Robbe-Grillet notes in *Sur le Choix des Générateurs*, all nations and all religions, sooner or later, claim that their system of values is natural and God-given: "For the first time, a mode of production announces itself as non-natural; . . the myth of the natural . . has been used by the social, moral and political order so as to establish and prolong itself. Bourgeois order, bourgeois morality and bourgeois values were supposed to be natural, i.e., inscribed in the order of things, and were therefore just, innocent and definitive. Narrative order was similarly viewed: it was not supposed to raise any questions concerning the origin and justification of its formal structures." (*159*)

Magritte's and Robbe-Grillet's art opposes all systems that emphasize their own inevitability. Their art subverts such norms while advocating the non-natural. Magritte's bowler-hatted man is his code image for the bourgeoisie.

His mistrust of the bourgeoisie has always been pronounced, even though he himself lived and dressed like a bowler-hatted man. This explains why he paints a man's face - the face is every man's identity - obscured by an apple (*The Great War*, 1964). Magritte has painted man's anonymity, his void, his emptiness, because, in essence, every bourgeois has the same face and each one can be identified by the ready-made. Magritte's pronouncements on this matter in *Ecrits Complets* are corrosive and aggressive. He goes beyond commonality to emphasize the stupidity, baseness, and duplicity of the bourgeois mind: "*We are merely the subjects of this so-called civilized world, in which intelligence, baseness, heroism and stupidity get on very well together and are alternately being pushed to the fore. We are the subjects of this incoherent, absurd world in which weapons are manufactured to prevent war, in which science is used to destroy, to construct, to kill, and to prolong the life of the dying, in which the most insane undertaking works against itself.*" (*EC 103*)

Magritte dramatizes the link between public performance and the private self, and, like Robbe-Grillet, he explores the latent eroticism of the creative act. Of course Freud was well aware of the sexual symbolism of writing, i.e., the releasing of a liquid from a pen onto blank paper, an act that he describes in *Project for a Scientific Psychology*. Derrida, in his study of Freud's "*Project*", interprets the word "*Bahnung*", a term referring to the economic relationships between various parts of the psyche, as a double image of the act of inscribing a text and of sexual penetration. Since Freud, the sexual connotations of the creative act in terms of pleasure, penetration, or gestation, have indeed become commonplace.

Magritte's 1936 drawing entitled *White Magic* (1936) is thoroughly consistent with the sexual symbolism of the creative act: it depicts a clothed man inscribing the word "*écrire*" on the abdomen of a reclining woman, as though she were "*the body of the text*". The pleasure that Barthes derives from such "*writerly*" endeavors is prefigured in Magritte's pencil drawing. In this context, it is fitting that *The Master of the*

In the Temple of Dreams

Revels (BC 123), who is "*enflamed*" by desire, should do his balancing act on the tightrope above the steps, between the phallic baluster and the phallic smokestack. For Magritte and Robbe-Grillet, as in Freud, the pleasure principle overrides the reality principle. Their act devalues realism in favor of specular pleasures. For example, the painting entitled *The Pleasure Principle* (1937) (*BC 100*), depicts a man dressed in a coat and tie sitting at a table. His right hand is on the table and his fingers are poised, as though to reach for and grab the stone-like object that looks like a meteorite. The man's head has been replaced by a pure, glowing incandescence - the principle of pure pleasure and consciousness. Says Magritte: "*Our mental universe is brightened by pleasure which we have chosen, like a sun, to guide us*" (*EC 223*). In *The Art of Living* (1967) a red sun has replaced the man's head. In *The Pleasure Principle*, the arm is the link between the meteorite on the table and the glowing head that is as bright as the sun. Since the sun, as Magritte has noted, is our origin (*EC 122*), a meteorite may be viewed as a fragment from the "*Big Bang*", the original explosion with which the universe began. The evolution of life from its earliest beginnings has culminated in man, a conscious being capable of experiencing pleasure as well as "*reflecting*" on pleasure.

Astrophysicist Hubert Reeves, in *Poussiere d'Étoiles*, says that the universe everywhere is composed of identical chemical elements and compounds. The history of the universe is the story of matter organizing itself along specific lines: particles, nuclei, the stars, the atoms, the molecules, the cells and living beings all belong to the same evolving continuum. From the initial Big Bang, during a period of approximately 15 billion years, there has been a "*logical*" organization of matter to produce life. Man, literally made up of star dust and human consciousness, is the triumphant end product of the organization of matter. Since consciousness is normally not visible, an art form that can materialize it is indeed magical. *The Pleasure Principle* re-creates, symbolically, the primordial emergence of organized matter.

The world as we know it has evolved trees that produce fruit, but why not also that produce birds (*Pleasure*) (1926). Magritte takes pleasure in exploiting the free field of creative possibilities outside the range of the "*normal*". If these possibilities are freed from their bonds and allowed to develop, a new reality emerges. It is the pleasure of creating different combinations that attracts and fascinates both Magritte and Robbe-Grillet. *The Pleasure Principle* links the artist's imagination with a universal force. The painting's incandescence, its fire, transmits to matter (through the position of the arm and hand) a primal urge of sexuality and pleasure that leads to the ultimate creative act: *The Beautiful Captive* (1947), i.e., reflexive art and the self-awareness of the text. The problem of self-awareness depends on two factors: *Of what is one aware?* and, *Whose awareness is it?* These questions cancel each other out in the intuition that the self exists. All levels of consciousness are capable of suddenly reducing to this luminous point. *The Pleasure Principle*, when

In the Temple of Dreams

joined with *The Beautiful Captive*, gives us the intuition of consciousness as a creative act that points to itself as a creative act. This is the luminous point.

When we recall that Robbe-Grillet begins his novel with the falling meteorite (*The Castle of the Pyrénées*) (1959), that the novel devotes itself to the pursuit of pleasure, that Robbe-Grillet's interest is in the story of telling and not in the telling of a story, then the consciousness of the creative act and the reflexive structures that transmit this consciousness to the reader, constitute the artist's goal. Says Magritte: "*Thought is light*" (*EC 391*). This is "*the pleasure principle*" of writing, of the *"writerly"* text, of "*flaming fiction*". Magritte's painting, The Pleasure Principle, is its code-image.

Pleasure is indeed an essential dimension of the "*writerly*" text. In his pursuit of "*bliss*" (Barthes' "*jouissance*"), Robbe-Grillet has included five Magritte paintings oriented "*toward pleasure*". They are: *The Depths of Pleasure* (1948) (*BC 61*), *The Pleasure Principle* (*BC 100*), *The Master of the Revels* (*Le maître du plaisir, BC 123*), *Pleasure* (*BC 124*), and *Toward Pleasure* (1950) (*BC 134*). Says Magritte: "*When we deliberately chose pleasure as life's supreme goal, we already had twenty years of surrealism behind us*" (*EC 223*). The last sentence of Robbe-Grillet's novel echoes Magritte: "*Once more something urges me out of myself toward pleasure*" (BC 150). The novel begins with a falling stone and ends with the word "*pleasure*", even as *A la Recherche du Temps Perdu* begins and ends with the word "*time*". It would seem that pleasure is as significant a *leitmotif* for Magritte and Robbe-Grillet as time was for Proust. We should also keep in mind Barthes' analysis of artistic orgasm in *The Pleasure of the Text*, a form of bliss that Robbe-Grillet and Magritte both pursue in order to "*possess*" their beautiful captives. Says Robbe-Grillet: "*The hunt resumes once again. Already, at the far end of the long corridor, enclosed in a remote room behind parallel, vertical bars, immobile, the beautiful prisoner, as yet untouched, smiles at me inexplicably from her cage.*" (*BC 15*)

It is significant that the adjectives "*vertical*" and "*immobile*" - adjectives that are used to describe the falling stone, the bars of the cell, and Anne-Marie - adjectives that appear in the opening and closing paragraphs of the novel, should reinforce Magritte's secret connection between stone and woman. Robbe-Grillet's descriptions support Magritte's portrayal of unusual affinities between the animate and the inanimate. Once again Anne, the mother, and Marie, the virgin, emphasize the self-restoring level of the text, a text that every reader approaches anew, as though it were virginal, "*untouched*", and as yet unpenetrated. *Anne-Marie and the Rose* (1961), although the painting is deliberately trite, sums up Robbe-Grillet's and Magritte's themes: the dramatization of art and the imagination, woman as mythic goddess, lunar cycles, nature's affinities, the sky, the moon, the sea, the rose, eggs, and stones. *Anne-Marie and the Rose* is an appropriate ending to the meta-fictional "*pleasures*" both artists have been pursuing.

In the Temple of Dreams

The novel thus ends with a resumption of "*the hunt*" for meaning, for a new captive, for a new text, for new and different pleasures. Throughout this relentless pursuit nothing has been left standing, neither bourgeois values nor the text: they are all abolished. Robbe-Grillet's description of the ruined city by the seashore corresponds to this undermining of reality and of expectation: "*When the windows nonetheless light up the silhouettes of the rare buildings that remain standing in this wasteland of work yards and ruins.*" (*BC 135*)

What *is* left standing is that other reality called art - that elusive entity that Magritte and Robbe-Grillet pursue through the labyrinth of things, words, images, and language. Through art and the artistic process, both men assert the primacy of the creative act to challenge nature and man's institutions. One of Robbe-Grillet's early essays was entitled *Nouveau Roman: Homme Nouveau*. Jacques Leenhardt compares this new man to a two-headed Janus looking both forward and backward (*160-61*). He is like the man in Magritte's painting *The Glass House* (*BC 52*), presenting a simultaneous view of his (Magritte's) face and the back of his head. Robbe-Grillet's fiction recapitulates the past, describes the present, and announces the future, even as Magritte's painting, *The Liberator* (1947), epitomizes the desire of both men to reshape the world in the image of "*the beautiful captive*".

This new art talks about itself in order to be itself. Its self-consciousness allows it to be simultaneously abstract and factual, absent and present, invisible and visible. It is both art and woman. Magritte's *The Beautiful Captive*, as a captive, denotes art and connotes woman. Robbe-Grillet's title and text denote woman and connote art. Together, painting and novel are the "*false mirrors*" (*The False Mirror*) of each other's intentions and fulfilments. "*Elle, aile, belle*" provide the necessary slippages of meaning. "*She*" is the *Idol* (1965), rising like the Phoenix from the ashes of *The Backfire* (1943). "*She*" is the picture of consciousness that links stone and woman by means of *The Pleasure Principle*. The parthenogenetic egg generates the permutations and bifurcations of the artistic dialogue between text and image that is *The Beautiful Captive*.

———————————————————

5. A Sojourn in the Maison de Rendez-Vous
Dreamplay in Robbe-Grillet

Professor Roch C. Smith
(University of North Carolina, Greensboro)

Having learned from Robbe-Grillet that the working title for a film in progress, *Le Retour de Franck*, was being abandoned in favour of *Un Bruit Qui Rend Fou*, I had anticipated the film's English title as *A Maddening Noise*. Predictions on a work in progress are inherently risky, although Robbe-Grillet's previous titles had been rendered more or less literally into English. Yet *The Blue Villa*, the concise and evocative title given to the English version of Robbe-Grillet's and Dimitri De Clercq's 1995 film *Un Bruit Qui Rend Fou*, turns out to be especially appropriate, since a house of pleasure called the Blue Villa serves as a central visual and verbal point of reference in this film shot largely on the Greek island of Hydra.

The Blue Villa also relates intertextually to another Blue Villa on an island - Lady Ava's house of assignation in Hong Kong from *La Maison de Rendez-vous*. Robbe-Grillet indicates that the objective reference for *The Blue Villa* was Victoria Ocampo's house in Argentina as well as a former bordello in Shanghai. But the name might apply to another real place, namely the building occupied by his publisher, *Les Editions de Minuit*, whose titles and logo are blue and whose building at 7 rue Bernard-Palissy, is a former bordello that still has double entry doors each with its own peephole. Indeed, Robbe-Grillet is fond of saying that his office at Minuit was the voyeur's room.

When Thieu, the Police Chief in the film *The Blue Villa*, absently drops his copy of Robbe-Grillet's *Les Derniers Jours de Corinthe* with its recognizable Minuit cover onto his desk, the viewer is given still another suggestion about possible connections among these blue villas. Together the several blue villas serve as a meeting place, a virtual "maison de rendez-vous" for the filmic and verbal narratives belonging to the latter half of Robbe-Grillet's career. Often referred to as post-modern works, these narratives include the so-called "new new novels", beginning with *La Maison de Rendez-vous*, the autobiographical trilogy or "auto-fictions", the last of which was *Les Derniers Jours de Corinthe* and, I would argue, all of his films since *Trans-Europ-Express*. The latter appeared in 1966, the year after *La Maison de Rendez-vous*. Since then, neglected villas and virtually abandoned buildings have figured prominently in much of Robbe-Grillet's work, as if the mirrored and stuccoed facades of the hotel in *L'Année Dernière à Marienbad* had been allowed to fall into disrepair. One thinks of the castle in *L'Homme Qui Ment*, the factory and Tunisian house in *L'Eden et Après*, the dungeons in *Glissements Progressifs du Plaisir*, the sometime abandoned villa in the film *La Belle Captive*, as well as decaying interior spaces in much of his fiction, from the New York subways and apartment buildings in *Projet pour une Revolution à New York*, the cells in *Topologie d'une Cité Fantôme*,

In the Temple of Dreams

the subterranean passages in *Souvenirs du Triangle d'Or*, and the apartments and damp meeting places in *Djinn*. I will leave for another time a consideration of the role of the house or villa in all these works and will focus here on the 1966 film *Trans-Europ-Express* and the 1965 novel *La Maison de Rendez-vous* as important precursors to Robbe-Grillet's film, *The Blue Villa*.

Robbe-Grillet frequently launches filmic narrative by using what I have called "imagistic generators". External to the flow of images that constitute the film's diegesis, the imagistic generator initiates subsequent narrative through an apparent intrusion that usually finds it's source in the repertoire of publicly recognizable icons. Whether it be the reprise of Marcel DuChamp's art in *L'Eden et Après*, or the false Magritte in *La Belle Captive*, the imagistic generator, when viewed from a diegetic perspective, seems to appear "ex nihilo".

In Trans-Europ-Express such "external" images are exaggerated to the point of parody when Trintignant, carrying a gun in a hollowed out book entitled *Transes*, stops at a news-stand where he slips a pornographic magazine called *Europe* into a copy of the news weekly, *L'Express*. From these images will come not only the title of the film but, apparently, the story itself: a story of underworld figures involved in transporting contraband across the borders of northern Europe on the express train. Yet this story is indeed a caricature, as is made clear by the even more exaggerated credits sequence where an excited voice-over describes what the viewer sees: Jean-

Louis Trintignant, wearing a patently false beard, carrying a round, comic-strip bomb with a burning fuse, pursued by men in trenchcoats. Thus is the viewer put on notice from the very beginning that the imagistic sources of this film's non-linear narration, like the apparent story itself, are suspect. Functioning as a *mise en abyme* or interior duplication of the generating device within a story, these and other ostensibly generating sequences only appear to be generating and synthesizing points for this particular story.

Robbe-Grillet makes a similar use of *mise en abyme* in *The Blue Villa*, where paintings on the villa walls appear to generate narrative threads. Thus a painting depicts the ghostly Frank on his boat in the middle of a storm before Fred Ward, the actor playing Frank, is shown on the bow of his Chinese junk facing the crashing waves, like Wagner's Flying Dutchman. Frank's return aboard the junk has already been shown in an opening scene and indeed the rumor (*bruit* in French) of his return is the talk of the town - one reason for the title, *Un Bruit Qui Rend Fou*. Nothing, then, is really generated by this painting. Indeed, the "live" scene of Frank on the bow is manifestly artificial so that the viewer is presented, in effect, with a *mise en abyme* of a *mise en abyme* and the imagistic generator is reduced to a decorative remnant. It is as artificial as Trintignant's beard at the opening of *Trans-Europ-Express* or as the apparent link between that film's narrative and the discussions in the compartment among Jean (Robbe-Grillet), Lucette (Catherine Robbe-Grillet), and Marc (Paul Louyet).

In the Temple of Dreams

With the imagistic generator having been undermined in both *Trans-Europ-Express* and *The Blue Villa*, a related yet distinctive image - the synoptic image - serves to advance the narrative. The synoptic image's suggestive and narrative power relies on a paradoxical combination of subtlety and visual impact. Like the imagistic generator, the synoptic image engenders narrative through striking visual means, but, unlike the imagistic generator, it is not external. It grows out of the diegesis, and summarizes both narrative and structural features of the film. It's significance comes from its power to act as both visual catalyst and synthesizer. The term "synoptic image" refers to this ability to offer both an optical instigation and summation of the narrative.

An early instance of the use of this image in *Trans-Europ-Express* occurs when Jean, the director, manipulates the train's window blind. While screen and window are often connected metaphorically, in visual terms this window is remarkably similar to a film screen in proportion and appearance. Its role as a generator and summarizer of this particular film's story is underscored by its ability to link inside and outside through this screen-like "looking-glass". Indeed, the allusion to Lewis Carroll's tale is strengthened by the many shots of mirrors within the compartment - all contributing to what Raylene Ramsay has called the "specular technique" (145) of this film. The synoptic function of this image is further emphasized by its metonymical link to the train of the title.

Trans-Europ-Express, then, is not so much a film noir about cops and gangsters - although it replicates the look of that genre - but is, rather, a story of narration in which travelling and narration are inter-related. The train functions as both a vehicle and a metaphor for telling a story, a story that is often fragmented and frequently goes off the prescribed track. In this narrative of a voyage which is really a voyage of narration, the image of the train window, like the film screen, generates story and structure through transparency, and mirror inversion. This story will lead to the hotel "Miro" in "Anvers", the city of mirrors and inversions humorously alluded to by Trintignant as "Anvers et Endroit".

The metaphor of travel as narrative, generated through this early synoptic image of the train window, is opposed by the stasis and isolation of the city. When the story being narrated from the compartment moves from the train to the city of Antwerp, the film focuses upon suspended action - temporary dwellings or stopping points as well as industrial sights and sounds that seem to belie any human presence. Here, for instance, ships rarely move - they are in dry dock or at anchor - and the ponderous loading cranes are motionless among the debris of the shipyard. The locus of action may also shift to the hotel, the house, the terminal, the street monument. These too are static locations, where travel may begin or end but is currently suspended. While encounters between characters do occur, they are invariably relationships of commerce and power: the prostitute and her client, himself a sadist; the agent

In the Temple of Dreams

in training and the organization; gangsters and the police. The only exception to such crass relationships is the meeting between Trintignant, in his role as Elias, and an adolescent boy, a waiter in a local café. At first Elias is overtly suspicious of the boy, who like Elias, is a wanderer from Paris who lives alone in Antwerp. But when the young waiter selflessly offers Elias a refuge from his pursuers, a bond quickly develops between these two solitary figures. While the exact nature of their relationship is never made explicit (there is a suggestion that theirs' is a homosexual encounter, for example), what is clear is that Elias takes on a narrator's role. He recounts a tale of adventure to his young protector and promises to bring back books of adventure stories on his next trip to Paris, again linking narration and travel.

The synoptic image for the Antwerp sequences, and, it can be argued, for the entire film, is the adolescent's house. Standing alone in a wasteland of cleared urban lots, it serves as an apt metaphor for the stark isolation of its sole inhabitant and of the alienation of the other characters in the city. Inside hang film-related pictures (James Bond, Jean-Paul Belmondo, an American Indian, etc.). Some, like the hand-made drawings of flowers and crude guns on the fogged over window, suggest graffiti. Indeed, Robbe-Grillet has admitted that he himself was the graffiti artist, having included, among the drawings, the phone number of *Les Editions de Minuit!* But, whatever their actual source, within the diegesis these hand-made drawings parallel the fleeting images from popular culture on the wall. Both sets of images point to the adolescent's longing for stories, for meaning, however tenuous - a longing Trintignant satisfies by telling the boy an adventure story not unlike the one the viewer has been witnessing. Elias could not have given a more fitting response to the generosity of his young rescuer than to tell him stories and to promise to bring him back more stories when he returns from his next trip to Paris. Despite the shattered world in which he moves, Elias keeps his word and returns with several books of adventure tales. His act underscores the importance of story-telling in the film. Narrative movement gives momentary meaning to what is otherwise an environment of mistrust and alienation.

As a synoptic image the adolescent's house is complex in that it is really a nucleus of images. Like the adolescent himself, it seems, at first glance, to stand outside the more obvious narrative of drug-running, prostitution, sadism and murder. Yet, there are frequent reminders that such stories, like those surrounding the adolescent, are artificial, including the film's ending when Trintignant and Marie-France Pisier step out of character and resume their "real" identities. These bits of artificial narratives are the underlying contraband of the film. The gangster-like characters deal in the drug of conventional narration, including Trintignant who "smuggles" stories back to Antwerp on the *Trans-Europ-Express*. The house, standing starkly alone, both visually and narratively, engenders and summarizes the story-telling that swirls around it. It relates what the film is about by clarifying the underlying of narration as contraband in the film.

In the Temple of Dreams

If we turn now to *La Maison de Rendez-vous*, we see that the reader is faced with a veritable kaleidoscope of narrative sequences including elegant soirées with private theatrical skits for special guests at Lady Ava's Blue Villa, a beautiful Eurasian woman walking a mastif, a mannequin of a beautiful woman walking a mastif, a street sweeper gazing at the cover of an erotic magazine, Sir Ralph Johnson, known as "The American", falling madly for the beautiful prostitute Lauren and chasing all over Hong Kong to find enough money to take her away, the suicide, or murder, of Marchant, Lauren's fiancé, the procurement and delivery of a mysterious brown envelope filled with packets of drugs (or perhaps a manuscript), the encounter with the Chinese intermediary Tchang, the meetings with the elusive and presumably rich Edouard Manneret, also known as "le Vieux", the stories of scandalous events that have occured in Hong Kong recounted by an unnamed red-faced fat man, and the first-person narrative that opens the novel with a confession that woman's flesh has always played a great role in his dreams.

Yet the metaphor of a kaleidoscope does not do justice to this work, in which inside and outside often flow into each other so smoothly that they are readily confused, where common reality turns into theatre, and theatre into reality, and where space can seem so amorphous that it can grow or shrink in size. Bruce Morrissette has suggested that Robbe-Grillet's non-linear narratives represent Möbius strips or Klein bottles because of the way they fold in and turn back upon themselves. Such an image translates Robbe-

Grillet's narrative convolutions far better than that of a constantly changing but flat kaleidoscope. Yet certain key features of *La Maison de Rendez-vous* are not adequately accounted for by either comparison.

While it may easily go unnoticed, Robbe-Grillet's narrator indicates in the very first sentence, alluded to above, that this novel is concerned with dreams. There are, within the narrative, numerous instances of dream-like sequences in which, for example, Kim searches for Tchang in an apartment building only to encounter a false Tchang and to open an apartment door onto a large meeting hall before descending the stairs so rapidly that she is soon engaged in a fall worthy of Alice in Wonderland. Ralph Johnson's mad trek around Hong Kong in search of money, while he himself is followed by police, has a nightmarish quality, as does Kim's inability to scream when confronted by a mysterious figure in the stairway. On other occasions narrative sequences are specifically introduced as "scenes" or with words such as *maintenant* and *à present* stressing discontinuity and immediacy, as in a dream. Many of these scenes return, often with minor changes, with obsessive regularity. And somehow, in the midst of this whirlwind, the *Blue Villa* emerges as a place of some permanence, seemingly the only place that can hold the centrifugal narrative together.

Here, as in *Trans-Europ-Express*, place - specifically a house - emerges as the eye in a storm of motion, madness and hysteria involving outlandish plots of drug smuggling, prostitution, sado-eroticism, murder etc. At the centre of a narrative web, the *Blue Villa*

In the Temple of Dreams

serves as the focal point of dreams, whether those of the narrator, the several characters who at various times become narrators themselves, or ultimately, of the reader who responds to the novel's invitation to dream.

Gaston Bachelard describes just such a centre of oneiric activity when he speaks of space and the dream house. For Bachelard - who like Robbe-Grillet is a man of science turned literary dreamer - common reality is transformed by imagination and reverie. A corner can become a universe as space expands or shrinks in response to the daydreamer's imagination. The realist's distinctions between inside and outside can melt away. This may be the stuff of surrealism, as many have suggested, but as Raylene Ramsay has argued in the case of Robbe-Grillet, and as I have pointed out with respect to Bachelard, the source of such imaginings is to be found largely in the transformation of common reality indicated by contemporary microphysics and non-Euclidean geometry. Bachelard called his attraction to reveries of pleasant space a "topophilia". Topophilia characterizes the pleasure derived from playing with images of space; it describes a ludic, as opposed to a rationalist approach to space.

That Robbe-Grillet, a former agricultural engineer and statistician, and the author of the mathematically inspired but oneiric *Topologies d'une Cité Fantôme*, should engage in "topophiliac" narratives should come as no surprise. After all, Robbe-Grillet has long been fond of incorporating games into his work - a feature that continues with his use of Mah-Jongg games in *The Blue Villa*. Yet the ludic quality of space was initially hidden by his radically geometric descriptions. *La Maison de Rendez-vous* differs from Robbe-Grillet's early fiction largely because its narrative plays with space in such a free and aleatory way that the game has no discernible rules.

The ubiquity of spatial play and the title itself pose the question of the role of the *Blue Villa* within this topophiliac narrative. The ready assumption upon reading this work is that the *Maison* of the title refers to the *Blue Villa*. But is the *Blue Villa* the "Maison de Rendez-vous"? It is certainly "the house of assignation" (the title given to the English translation) where Lady Ava, Ralph Johnson, Lauren, the red-faced fat man, Kim, and even the Hong Kong police all meet. But, much as in a dream, there is a protean quality to the spaces of the *Blue Villa*. The narrator may describe a scene that suddenly becomes a stage, or a stage play for customers with special tastes may shift to a street scene.

In parallel fashion, the identity of the characters themselves is far from fixed. Is Sir Ralph really an American, is he a British Lord, is he Edouard Manneret's son, is his name Johnson, Johnston, Jonstone, Jonestone? Is the woman who runs the *Blue Villa* Lady Ava, Eva Bergmann, Eve, a stylish, fairly young woman, an old and dying lady? What should the reader make of the real and the false Tchang, who in every respect except for the admission of being an intermediary, are exactly the same? Who is the old man who makes noise with his steel-tipped cane upstairs, at times *chez* Manneret, at

In the Temple of Dreams

times *chez* Lady Ava? The narrator calls him Boris or "le roi Boris", a name Robbe-Grillet had used in *Un Régicide*, his first novel, completed in 1949 but not published until 1978, so not yet known to the readers of *La Maison de Rendez-vous*. Who is Edouard Manneret? Is he a painter - Edouard Manet, perhaps - a rich Hong Kong business man, a smuggler, a writer? All these possibilities are suggested in the text. Intertextual allusions provide even more alternatives. Is Edouard Manneret modelled after Mallarmé at his writing table, or after the mysterious Henri de Corinthe, as Robbe-Grillet suggests in *Le Miroir Qui Revient*. Since Edouard, alias "le Vieux", alias "le roi Boris" mistakes Johnson for his son, should we see a connection between Edouard Manneret and Jean, alias Boris in Robbe-Grillet's 1968 film *L'Homme Qui Ment*?

Does the identity of the characters really matter at all when it so readily shifts? If much of the narrative takes place in the *Blue Villa*, much of it also is located on the streets of Hong Kong, in the Kowloon district, at the Hotel Victoria, on the ferry. Edouard Manneret, who seems a key figure, as a writer, as the object of Ralph Johnson's search, and as the victim of a murder that is recounted some four times, each with a different murderer, is never seen in the *Blue Villa*, except when played by an actor. Nor is the mysterious Tchang, the object of Kim's own search. *La Maison de Rendez-vous* thus refers to the entire novel and not just to the *Blue Villa*. The novel itself is the house where all the characters in their various guises meet. The *Blue Villa*, as a house of dreams within the diegesis, synthesizes and catalyzes the house of dreams that is the novel. Like the isolated house in *Trans-Europ-Express*, the *Blue Villa* stands out as a focal point where the narrative strands converge. As such, it too serves as a synoptic image, but, also like the house in *Trans-Europ-Express*, it is not the whole story. The house in *Trans-Europ-Express*, is isolated and threatened by urban renewal. Figuratively, the *Blue Villa* is also built upon a shaky foundation. Not only are the characters who occupy it and the villa itself protean, but its very existence is questionable, a dependency of the oft-used conditional of conjecture in this novel's narrative.

The conditional of conjecture figures prominently in that other *Blue Villa* that is Robbe-Grillet's 1995 film. Here another Edouard, Edouard Nord, repeatedly proposes narrative threads that might hide his culpability in the death of his stepdaughter, Santa, while Thieu, the Police Chief, dictates his own narrative of conjecture that would reveal Nord's guilt. As in *La Maison de Rendez-vous*, other narrators are at work as well, until Edouard Nord, a pretender like his novelistic predecessor and probable alter-ego, Edouard Manneret, alias Boris (Gudonov), alias Henri de Corinthe, weaves enough narrative thread to ensnare himself, like a spider caught and self-devoured in his own web - an image of the narrator Robbe-Grillet specifically proposes in *Les Derniers Jours de Corinthe*.

The narrative of *La Maison de Rendez-vous*, with its repeated depiction of the erotic magazine cover turned over by a street sweeper, reminds the reader

In the Temple of Dreams

that the entire edifice, not only of the *Blue Villa*, but of the novel entitled *La Maison de Rendez-vous* is a product of the imagination, a fiction. Thus, this convoluted narrative can be ascribed to the imaginings of the street sweeper, or someone observing him, for whom the erotic magazine cover, like Proust's tea-soaked *madeleine*, becomes the foundation for the novel the reader has before him.

Robbe-Grillet's close descriptions of objects and spatial relationships won him the sobriquet of "*choisiste*" for his early fictions. The view of a coldly objective Robbe-Grillet became so well-established in the popular press that his affirmation in *Le Miroir Qui Revient* that he had never spoken of anything but himself was problematic for some. Yet the notion that Robbe-Grillet's work presented an objectivity of surfaces was already seriously weakened by Robbe-Grillet's own narrative practice, including the increasingly central role of eroticism and the use of oneiric structures. Bachelard's topophilia recognized that, unlike the subjectively neutral space of geometry, imagined space always acquires a quality for the imagining subject. The subjective quality of imagined space in Robbe-Grillet's filmic and fictional narratives comes to the fore as the growing eroticism of his work suggests that imagined, narrative space is to be played with and enjoyed. In moving from the geometric, labyrinthine settings of his early novels to the topophiliac dream-play of his post-modern work, Robbe-Grillet continues to use space as the medium for his explorations of the imagination. The difference is that space is now more obviously subjective, despite his continued use of precise description. With *La Maison de Rendez-vous* Robbe-Grillet transforms the seemingly objective realism of his early novels into a subjective idealism that, as it turns out, no voyeur of surfaces had ever quite managed to erase. The world thus revealed is a *Blue Villa*, a temple of dreams, constructed by the ghostly shadows of shifting characters ceaselessly weaving their narrative webs. When, as in Robbe-Grillet's film *The Blue Villa*, their narrative games can actually be heard, it is indeed a maddening noise.

---

6. Texte, Film et Code:
Dysnarration et Cohérence

Professor Pierre Van den Heuvel
(Université de Nimègue, Holland)

O. Préliminaires

J'ai choisi de consacrer mon propos à un aspect essentiel de l'oeuvre d'Alain Robbe-Grillet: ce qu'on peut appeler d'une manière générale le "*Brouillage*" que l'auteur-cinéaste instaure dans son oeuvre par des procédés très divers (glissements des niveaux narratifs, mélange du réel et de l'imaginaire, etc.) et qui subvertit les prescriptions des codes traditionnels des genres.

Ce faisant, je centrerai ma réflexion sur un sujet plus précis qui est le statut des personnages. On le sait, dans un récit textuel ou filmique, le personnage est l'élément le plus sûr, le plus stable, le plus solide dans la construction de l'univers fictionnel, celui qui est au centre de l'histoire narrée, qui la fait progresser et qui, grâce à la possibilité d'identification qu'il offre, permet de réaliser l'illusion réaliste chez le lecteur-spectateur. Or, Robbe-Grillet, sorcier au temple des rêves, grand-maître en dysnarration, réussit à ébranler le statut apparemment immuable du personnage, à déstabiliser son identité et, par là, à faire vaciller celles des interlocuteurs que nous sommes. Comment le fait-il? Et, surtout, dans quel but?

Pour cet aspect dans les textes littéraires, je référerai aux trois tomes des "*Romanesques*", notamment à *Angélique ou l'Enchantement* (1988); pour ce qui est de l'oeuvre cinématographique, je prendrai mes exemples dans *Trans-Europ-Express* (1966).

Une dernière précision, plûtot un avertissement: je ne suis pas un spécialiste de cinéma: que certains d'entre vous me pardonnent d'entrer sur leur terrain que j'exploiterai, quant à moi, dans la perspective d'une poétique de l'énonciation en utilisant les acquis de l'analyse discursive, narratologique et sémiotique.

A. TEXTE

Observons d'abord le phénomène du "brouillage" dans les textes littéraires.

Ici, l'originalité du discours robbe-grilletien résulte avant tout du traitement de l'histoire racontée qui est toujours multiple, incomplète, morcelée, nettement subordonnée à l'acte de parole: la représentation de la difficile mise en mots domine toujours celle des péripéties d'une éventuelle histoire. De plus, la narration elle-même se fonde le plus souvent sur l'ambiguïté d'instances énonciatives variables dont chacune se scinde volontiers en plusieurs sujets à statuts mobiles, voire interchangeables. Cette diversification des niveaux discursifs et narratifs déstabilise le lecteur qui s'attend à un récit "logique", fondé sur une causalité événementielle et psychologique, où la fiction se prête à être transformée en une pseudo-réalité que le lecteur s'approprie.

In the Temple of Dreams

Pour caractériser ce discours romanesque nouveau, on a souvent employé le terme de "dysnarration", qualification inadéquate, bien entendu, puisque le préfixe *dys-*, fréquemment utilisé en médecine, désigne - je cite le *Robert* - "le mauvais fonctionnement", "être en mauvais état" de quelque chose. Si je reprends ici, un peu ironiquement, ce terme, c'est pour deux raisons. D'abord, parce que cette dénomination réfère au *code* de réception, à une pratique de la lecture qui se fonde sur des conventions: la narration de ce type ne fonctionne pas bien par rapport à la réglementation littéraire en vigueur. Deuxièmement, parce que ce vocable a pris un sens bien précis dans le discours de certains critiques qui étudient le rapport entre le littéraire et le cinématographique. Ainsi, par exemple, dans *Récit écrit, Récit filmique* (1989), Francis Vanoyé définit la dysnarration de la manière suivante: "D'une façon générale, la dysnarration instaure des ruptures entre la fiction et la narration, dé-diégétisant cette dernière pour la ramener du coté de l'énonciation." Ce sont en effet des "ruptures" dans le récit et dans ses éléments constitutifs qui causent le brouillage dont j'ai parlé, cette confusion labyrinthique à laquelle l'auteur-cinéaste s'efforce de remédier en secourant son lecteur-spectateur par l'extension de ses interventions métadiscursives et réflexives.

1. Les Niveaux Discursifs

Quand on observe l'oeuvre autobiographique des "*Romanesques*" (*Le Miroir qui Revient*, 1984; *Angélique, ou l'Enchantement*, 1988; *Les Derniers*

Jours de Corinthe, 1994), on constate que le discours se distingue d'abord par la mise en commun de deux sujets habituellement bien distincts, donc par l'ambiguïté d'une double situation énonciative. D'un côté, il y a le sujet réel, l'écriv*ant* (Alain Robbe-Grillet), rapporteur des péripéties de la vie (c'est le sujet unique de l'autobiographie traditionelle); de l'autre, il y a le sujet poétique, l'écriv*ain*, transcripteur de l'activité imaginative. Non seulement ces instances aiment se mêler l'une à l'autre, mais encore elles se plaisent à changer constamment leur statut et leur identité. Cette pluralité des sujets et des situations énonciatives a des conséquences graves sur le plan de la réception: déstabilisé par cette procédure inhabituelle, le lecteur n'est plus à même de distinguer entre le compte rendu réaliste et l'invention fantasmatique, entre l'être et le paraître, entre le vrai et le faux. Car pour lui, l'écriture autobiographique, selon les conventions de la codification générique, doit constituer un discours de la réalité objective, de la véridiction, de la référentiation historique vérifiable.

Comment ces glissements des niveaux narratifs du réel et du fictionnel sont-ils réalisés dans *Angélique*? A l'extrême pôle du discours du réel se situe clairement un locuteur concret, la personne de l'auteur qui raconte sa vie; à celui du discours de fiction se trouve un narrateur, l'écrivain dans sa fonction de romancier, qui étale le produit de son imagination en six grandes séquences fonctionelles. Là où l'identification des sujets devient problématique, c'est entre ces deux pôles où elle dépend de l'interprétation du lecteur confus qui, pour pouvoir continuer sa lecture, se voit obligé d'occuper la place du sujet effacé, donc de s'associer au travail de la production.

2. Les Personnages

Il sera clair que la stratégie de la confusion des niveaux discursifs, fondés sur des sujets de parole, est étroitement liée à celle qui subvertit le statut des personnages, notamment de ceux qui sont aussi des instances locutrices à l'intérieur des deux grandes diégèses. Prenons quelques exemples. Dès la page 37 d'*Angélique*, le lecteur, pensant suivre le discours de l'auteur Robbe-Grillet - personnage réel, auto-diégétique, dont le discours n'est évidemment pas marqué par des guillemins - découvre tout à coup, grâce à des italiques, que le véritable locuteur est Henri de Corinthe, donc une instance fictive. Une confusion semblable est établie à la page 67 entre le texte de Robbe-Grillet et le prétendu manuscrit de Corinthe, maintenant à l'aide d'un dédoublement du pronom JE. Dans la première grande séquence fictionelle (p. 41-52), un dédoublement du pronom IL brouille le discours du père et du fils, incertitude encore rehaussée par la mention qu'il peut s'agir aussi d'une version apocryphe de Michelet. Plus spectaculaire encore est la perturbation au milieu de la vaste séquence centrale (pp.70-104) où le lecteur croit suivre le discours du romancier lorsqu'on lui apprend qu'il est en train de lire le journal de Corinthe, donc d'un personnage interne, ce qui le force à changer radicalement sa position de lecteur et même à reconsidérer le sens de la partie qu'il vient de lire.

Il va de soi que de tels audacieux brouillages discursifs et identitaires risquent fort d'éloigner le lecteur égaré dans ce "pays de pertes"! Robbe-Grillet, avec la générosité qu'on lui connaît, s'empresse alors d'intervenir pour rétablir le contact, soit par des paragraphes métadiscursives, soit par des stratégies de séduction. Dans le dernier cas cité, par exemple, la déstabilisation dangereuse est immédiatement suivie par l'extraordinaire *mise en abyme* du chant de la petite fauvette qui nous séduit non seulement par sa forme poétique, mais nous renseigne aussi sur la nature musicale du texte que nous lisons (p.88-89).

Dans les exemples observés, l'incertitude concernant le personnage-locuteur résulte de la fusion de deux instances d'énonciation, de deux sujets différents. L'inverse est également possible: la scission d'un même sujet en plusieurs instances distinctes, manoeuvre qui entraîne la transformation de l'identité du personnage. Ce deuxième stratagème, au caractère schizophrénique et aux effets déroutants, consiste en une construction syntaxique très rare, déjà présenté dans *La Belle Captive* et dans *Djinn*, qui transforme le statut grammatical du personnage: JE>IL, JE>VOUS, IL >JE, etc. Dans *Angélique*, l'auteur recourt à cette fiigure excessive dans les trois dernières séquences fictives. Après avoir déstabilisé le lecteur par la confusion discursive (l'effacement des frontières entre discours du réel et discours de fiction), par la confusion narrative (l'aplanissement des niveaux diégétiques) et par la confusion descriptive (la ressemblance quasi totale des figures de

In the Temple of Dreams

Corinthe, du père de Robbe-Grillet), l'auteur ose faire emploi de ce moyen choc pour ébranler la dernière résistance de son lecteur.

Le premier cas se présente à la page 120, dans la séquence "russe" où Corinthe et Manrica sont poursuivis par des loups, scène angoissante, racontée à la troisième personne, mais où, au moment le plus dramatique, le IL de Corinthe se transforme en JE dans la phrase: "Manrica, glacée de peur, se serre toujours plus étroitement contre *ma* poitrine . . Elle murmure . . des mots que *je* comprends à peine." D'abord raconté du dehors par un narrateur implicite, le récit se dramatise fortement non seulement par son contenu événementiel mais surtout par le passage de la narration impersonelle à un discours personnel très subjectivé. Le sujet JE, soumis à la force extraordinaire de la vision intense, s'identifie au héros au point de prendre sa place. Cette identification sert d'exemple au lecteur en acte qui, déjà bouleversé par les glissements narratifs, est invité à effectuer la même transformation. Cependant, au moment même où il est entraîné dans "l'enchantement" de cette aventure, jouissant à plein de l'effet du réel - cet idéal du roman traditionnel -, l'auteur l'arrache à cette position confortable en lui apprenant que la scène des loups n'est qu'une fabulation générée par l'observation d'une gravure de magazine.

Le deuxième cas se trouve à la page 138, dans la séquence fictionelle où Corinthe trouve un soldat français tué par un Uhlan prussien, Frédéric de Boncourt. Cette scène est racontée à la troisième personne, au présent de l'indicatif jusqu'au moment où l'officier allemand rend "un cérémonieux salut de parade" à Corinthe. Je cite: "Avec lenteur, l'inconnu relève enfin ses grands yeux clairs en direction du *capitaine français* (= Corinthe) qui vient d'apparaître, interrompant comme à regret sa méditation. Puis, dans un large mouvement souple et régulier d'une perfection d'épure, qui paraît avoir été tourné au ralenti (= référence au cinéma), il dégaine son sabre pour en présenter le métal nu verticalement devant son visage, menton levé, le tranchant de l'acier exposé face à *moi* . ." Comme cela est attesté par la suite, IL et JE désignent ici la même identité, celle du comte Henri de Corinthe. Mais l'opération pronominale implique la disparition du narrateur impersonnel et permet, à la page 142, une deuxième transformation identitaire: JE devient ici l'auteur lui-même. Ici encore, l'illusion est, peu après, rompue par la révélation du "générateur" de la scène, le tableau symboliste. L'aide au lecteur est apportée sous la forme d'un métatexte reliant l'écriture à l'activité militaire et à la representation théâtrale.

Le dernier exemple figure à la page 146, après le suicide de Simon. Ici, JE s'applique successivement à Corinthe, au narrateur et à Robbe-Grillet lui-même avant de se transformer en IL. Dans ce cas, la variation pronominale permet de se présenter deux fois : une scène très dramatique, celle de la mort d'Angélica et de Simon, racontée d'abord par le personnage intradiégétique de Boncourt, puis par un narrateur qui la transmet à la troisième personne. Cette opération soumet ainsi une même scène à

In the Temple of Dreams

plusieurs perspectives, ce qui oblige le lecteur à se déplacer, à se mobiliser et à accepter la trinité Corinthe-Boncourt-Père, instances-personnages qui sont assimilées peu à peu au JE de l'auteur réel dont ils ne sont que les *alter ego*.

Voyons maintenant comment cette technique du brouillage, qui s'attaque aux statuts classiques des niveaux narratifs et des personnages, est appliquée au cinéma.

B. FILM

Du point de vue narratologique, le film présente les mêmes éléments essentiels que le roman: il y a un récit, une histoire, une narration. Le "discours" cinématographique, au sens large du terme, procède cependant tout autrement quand il s'agit de faire fonctionner, par la mise en images, la représentation de ces éléments. Cela est évident, par exemple, pour la structuration du récit - le montage du visuel et du sonore - et du maniement des niveaux narratifs où la pronominalisation textuelle est remplacé par la présentation directe des locuteurs. La transformation d'un personnage en plusieurs identités (Corinthe, Boncourt, le père, l'auteur) où l'inverse n'est guère possible au cinéma traditionnel qui ne nous en présente que quelques exemples: le masque (de fer, et de Zorro) ou la transformation physique (Dr Jekyll and Mr Hyde, la grenouille changée en Prince Charmant). Pour brouiller les pistes le cinéaste Robbe-Grillet doit donc procéder autrement qu'en littérature. Prenons pour exemple le film *Trans-Europ-Express* (1966). D'abord, quel en est le système discursif?

1. Les Niveaux Narratifs

Le film raconte l'histoire d'un metteur en scène qui est en train de réaliser un film policier sur un transport de drogues entre Anvers et Paris (film dans le film, 8 1/2, Antonioni, etc.). L'originalité de ce film réside sans aucun doute, ici encore, dans la complexité des niveaux narratifs: plusieurs histoires plus ou moins élaborées, issues de sources variées, s'enchevêtrent. En schématisant, on peut distinguer, comme dans *Angélique*, deux grands niveaux: celui du "réel" (mais c'est évidemment un pseudoréel) et celui de la fiction. Le premier contient l'histoire du metteur en scène qui essaie de mettre au point le script du film qu'il est en train de tourner. Ce Jean, c'est Robbe-Grillet lui-même avec moustaches -, accompagné de Lucette, son épouse Catherine - et du producteur Marc. A l'intérieur de ce cadre, Jean et ses compagnons sont des narrateurs intradiégétiques (tandis que, dans la grande histoire du trafic de drogues ils sont extradiégétiques). Le deuxième niveau contient l'histoire policière avec Elias (Jean-Louis Trintignant) dans le rôle principal. Il va de soi que ces deux niveaux, dans leur totalité, sont dominés par un seul sujet d'énonciation, un narrateur inconnu, extradiégétique. Cette instance hiérarchiquement supérieure est directement responsable des séquences concernant l'équipe des cinéastes, séquences qui sont surtout situées au début et à la fin du film, et de la grande histoire centrale. En outre, elle est indirectement responsable des énoncés qui sont pris en charge par les locuteurs des deux niveaux. Il faut donc considérer le deuxième niveau, l'histoire du trafic de drogues, comme un récit enchâssé, au second degré, dont la responsabilité directe est déléguée au pauvre metteur-en-scène lequel, confronté à l'impossibilité de représenter une histoire cohérente, perd visiblement le contrôle de son film. C'est cette complexité formelle déroutante et cet échec de la recherche d'une cohérence logique qui font surgir peu à peu les questions fondamentales que pose *Trans-Europ-Express*: qu'est-ce que c'est que raconter? à quoi sert le récit? comment éviter l'illusion trompeuse de l'effet de réalisme? etc. . .

2. Le Statut des Personnages

Les glissements de ces deux niveaux narratifs s'observe le mieux à travers le fonctionnement des personnages. Pour subvertir l'identité de ceux-ci, le cinéma, qui montre les locuteurs à l'écran, ne peut pas se servir des stratégies linguistiques et poétiques que nous avons relevées dans *Angélique* (la transformation grammaticale, par exemple, est ici impossible).

Il est vrai que la parole peut contribuer à la confusion identitaire, mais cela donne vite dans la redondance ou dans l'invraisemblance, comme dans l'exemple suivant, tiré des *Glissements Progressifs du Plaisir* (1974):

Soupçonnée du meurtre de Nora, Alice reçoit en prison la visite de son avocate. Quand celle-ci entre, Alice s'exclame:

-- Nora!

L'Avocate: -- Comment?
Alice: -- Qui êtes-vous?
L'Avocate: -- Je suis votre avocate.
Alice: -- Vous ressemblez à Nora.

Ressemblance peu étonnante car le spectateur voit bien que les rôles de l'avocate et de Nora sont joués par la même actrice!!
Beaucoup plus fréquent et plus efficace est le procédé filmique de la déstabilisation du statut du personnage par un trucage spatio-temporel. Dans *L'Eden et Après* (1971), par exemple, des personnages regardent un documentaire sur la Tunisie, film qui, par voice-over, est commenté par l'un d'eux, Violette, que nous voyons également assise dans la salle. Sur l'écran apparaissent alors des personnages-acteurs identiques à ceux qui se trouve dans la salle de cinéma. Ce qui fait dire à André Gardies: "A la faveur du montage éclate une vive contradiction: Violette est douce du don d'ubiquité. Or, rien dans le contenu diégétique du film ne prépare cet événement et, mieux, rien dans la suite ne l'authentifie." (1981). Faute de montage? Non. La continuité des personnages est, au contraire, garantie par leur omni-présence; c'est l'illusion référentielle de l'espace et du temps qui est subvertie par des transitions transparentes et fluides qui mêlent le rêve à une "réalité" manifestement inventée.
Une telle organisation temporelle qui refuse la chronologie suivie et cohérente domine aussi, on se le rappelle, dans *L'Année Dernière à Marienbad* (1961) où elle réussit à effacer les frontières entre le vécu, l'imaginaire et le rêve.

In the Temple of Dreams

A ce propos, signalons encore l'opération ingénieuse, plus rare, par laquelle, dans *L'Immortelle* (1963), une chronologie "normale" est anéantie par l'utilisation très particulière d'attributs: pendant une scène apparemment suivi, le personnage porte des costumes différents, d'époques différentes (cf. *Djinn*, où la langue permet d'aller encore plus loin: un personnage y change de nature - se réifie ou s'anthropomorphise -, d'âge, de sexe même . . . En verbalisant on peut sans doute aller plus loin qu'en visualisant, pour des raisons bien diverses: je pense à certains thèmes comme l'androgynie, "le goût de la très jeune fille", etc.).

Mais remontons dans notre *Trans-Europ-Express* dont j'observais surtout l'incipit.

Dès le début du film, l'ambiguïté est installée: Jean, le metteur-en-scène du film à tourner, est également Alain Robbe-Grillet, metteur en scène du film *Trans-Europ-Exress*. Cette tension entre réalité et fiction, entre personne civile et acteur, déjà laconiquement établie par Hitchcock, est encore renforcée par l'apparition de Jean-Louis Trintignant, qui exécute une série d'actions que le metteur-en-scène avait consignées dans son script (échange de valise, montée dans le train). Le spectateur voit donc dans Trintignant l'*acteur* en train de jouer son rôle jusqu'au moment où il le voit entrer dans le compartiment des cinéastes! Le personnage de fiction redevient une personne, ce qui est confirmé par la script Lucette (Madame Robbe-Grillet) qui, après le départ de l'acteur, dit qu'il s'agit bien de Trintignant. La double référentialité, interne et externe, est troublante. Jean décide de donner à Trintignant le rôle principal de traficant de drogues et de l'appeler Elias. Nouvelle confusion par le moyen de la bande sonore qui fait entendre l'enregistrement sur cassette de la voix de Jean racontant l'histoire d'Elias, écoute illustré par les images de la première apparition de Trintignant (échange de valises, montée dans le train, etc.). Comme le lecteur d'*Angélique*, le spectateur ne sait plus s'il doit situer le récit au premier ou au deuxième niveau, s'il doit, pour réaliser son illusion, se situer dans la première ou dans la seconde diégèse. De plus, la scène de la fouille de la valise d'Elias s'accompagne sur la bande sonore d'une discussion entre Jean et Lucette sur le bien-fondé de la séquence, débat auquel le producteur Marc met fin en décidant de supprimer toute la séquence. Mais, entretemps, nous avons vu cette scène à deux reprises! La bande sonore est ici de grande importance: par son métadiscours enrégistré, le metteur en scène cherche par tous les moyens à justifier le maintien d'une image - peut-être inutile - que son imagination a engendrée. Pour lui, l'imaginaire l'emporte toujours sur la logique réaliste. Chateau/Jost commentent ainsi ce fragment: "Au lieu de reconstruire le monde diégétique en fonction de l'incongruité sémantique que Lucette lui signale, Jean en fait *varier* les éléments constitutifs et en premier lieu le statut des personnages."

Un autre cas semblable, situé bien plus loin, montre que cette lutte entre les deux niveaux narratifs ne tient aucunement compte de la logique du récit. Après avoir récupéré la clef, Elias reçoit l'ordre de

In the Temple of Dreams

Franck de transporter la valise d'Anvers à Paris. Il monte dans le train et cherche une place. A ce moment, on nous montre les cinéastes qui discutent dans leur compartiment. Réapparaît Elias qui cherche toujours pendant que la bande sonore reproduit la discussion du metteur-en-scène. La confusion est totale: l'homme qui cherche sa place, est-ce Elias ou Trintignant? le train se dirige-t-il vers Paris ou à Antwerp? On voit bien comment Robbe-Grillet, en jouant sur le temporel et le spatial, déstabilise non seulement le statut du personnage, mais aussi celui du spectateur.

Je reprends le début. Après la séquence qui suit la fouille de la valise, l'incertitude du discours narratif est illustré par l'image de rails et d'aiguillages qui figurent les directions et que pourrait prendre le récit. Le producteur propose de remplacer le transport de drogues par le trafic de diamants, mais Jean s'y oppose. Peu à peu, son histoire prend le dessus. Les commentaires techniques qui se font de plus en plus rares montrent que le metteur en scène ne parvient même plus à contrôler le cours des événements (le vol de la clef, par exemple). Une fois mise sur les rails, l'histoire lui échappe. Cela n'est pas de sa faute - si faute il y a! C'est la première instance narrative, extradiégétique, qui en porte la responsabilité, celle qui, comme nous l'avons vu, régit les deux diégèses en les distinguant selon les règles de l'art et du genre. Le metteur-en-scène Jean n'est que son valet ou plutôt sa victime. Faut-il donc considérer cette instance d'énonciation supérieure comme peu crédible, voire suspect? (Seymour Chatman a posé cette question en 1990). Non, car sa tâche n'est pas de rendre compte d'événements virtuels dans l'ordre de la logique codée, mais d'exposer artistiquement le produit de son invention. La question de la crédibilité ne peut donc se poser qu'au niveau des personnages-acteurs intradiégétiques dans les termes de la fameuse "vraisemblance". *Dans Le Narrateur au Cinéma* (1991), Robert Burgoyne formule ainsi les deux pôles de ce conflit: "Alors que chaque élément que construit le narrateur impersonnel est un fait qu'il concède au monde de la fiction, le personnage-narrateur doit mériter son autorité, et est toujours soumis à l'approbation ou au démenti d'une instance narrative supérieure." Il serait hasardeux d'appliquer de façon stricte cette formule aux films d'Alain Robbe-Grillet qui ont pour l'objet principal la lutte du pouvoir entre le discursif et le narratif d'un côté, et entre les diverses instances de l'énonciation de l'autre. Dans *Trans-Europ-Express*, par exemple, les interférences incessantes entre niveaux discursifs et les glissements indistinctes entre plans diégétiques s'opposent à une mise en place nette de la dichotomie en question. Ainsi, Jean est tantôt sujet tantôt objet de l'énonciation, tantôt destinateur tantôt destinataire, toujours confronté à cet autre "actant", l'histoire qui, se voulant autonome, semble poursuivre son propre chemin.

Pourtant, cette incertitude n'est qu'apparente. Elle n'existe pas pour le sujet de production qui en fait l'objet même de la représentation. Il faut relire ici ce que Robbe-Grillet dit lui-même de ce film dans *Angélique* (pp. 185-190): "Je savais exactement ce dont je désirais faire l'expérience . . . Je comprenais de mieux en mieux sur quels principes reposait le cinéma que j'avais en tête. D'abord ceci: la caméra ne dévoile pas la réalité, elle l'imagine. Et d'autre part, les tensions et les heurts dans le film ne se limitent pas aux effets de montage, ce sont tous les éléments du récit (caméra, éclairages, bruits, personnages, décors, actions, etc .) qui entrent en lutte sur l'écran." Et il précise: "Le couple classique créateur-création . . . s'y trouve sans cesse perturbé, inversé, éclaté dans des affrontements systématiques au sein du matériaux narratif . . . (les personnages) essayent tous. . . d'accaparer le pouvoir organisateur à l'intérieur du récit, dans le seul but de l'orienter suivant les préoccupations personelles, plus ou moins éloignées du projet initial." Ce thème du film, la mise en question de la narration classique à laquelle il faut ajouter le jeu avec les stéréotypes, n'a pas toujours été compris au début, ni par la critique qui y voyait surtout - je cite encore Robbe-Grillet - "un metteur en scène qui hésite et se perd au milieu des possibilités contradictoires de la création", ni par le public qui y trouvait l'occasion de voir exposée "l'imagerie secrète" de ses "fantasmes obscurs". Comme dans *Angélique*, cette mise en question est réalisée par la monstration des procédés cinématographiques employés, ce qui empêche l'illusion de se concrétiser, et par un métadiscours qui dénonce l'emprise des stéréotypes par une "exposition en trop vive lumière". Ainsi, comme le dit Georgio Cremonini, *Trans-Europ-Express* est "un récit métadiégétique, un modèle narratif qui se construit comme une réflexion sur la narration elle-méme" (1988). Dans ce sens, Robbe-Grillet inverse l'ordre du cinéma traditionnel où, au nom de l'illusion diégétique, le sujet de création s'efforce d'éliminer toute réflexion métadiscursive et toute référence à l'acte d'énonciation.

C. CONCLUSIONS

1. Le brouillage qui caractérise l'oeuvre littéraire et cinématographique d'Alain Robbe-Grillet est instauré, dans les deux formes d'art, par la subversion des mêmes éléments narratifs: les niveaux discursifs et le statut des personnages. Les procédés par lesquels les effets de confusion sont obtenus peuvent cependant différer. Ainsi, le changement d'une identité par la transformation pronominale est propre à l'écriture; la confusion obtenue par un déplacement spatio-temporel appartient plutôt au cinéma (il y a d'autres moyens filmiques, bien sûr, dont je n'ai pas parlé, comme les couleurs et la musique . .).

2. Les difficicultés qu'éprouve le lecteur-spectateur à suivre cette nouvelle narration textuelle et filmique sont allogées par l'insertion de séquences métadiscursives et de figures réflexives - e.g. la *mise en abyme* - qui réfèrent à l'intention de l'auteur-cinéaste.

3. La construction narrative originale (*Nouvelle Roman, Nouvelle Autobiographie, Cinéma d'Auteur*) a pour but d'instaurer un "ordre" nouveau. Cet ordre est fondé sur des principes qui font la cohérence de l'oeuvre: l'impossibilité de reproduire le réel, la primauté de l'imaginaire, la prédominance de l'énon-

ciation, la participation de l'interlocuteur au processus de création.

4. Cette conception nouvelle exige une abolition préalable de l'ordre ancien, rondé sur l'illusion du réel. D'une part, cette conversion des habitudes est obtenue par l'exposition du processus de production et par la dysnarration elle-même (les trous, les silences, les failles . .). D'autre part, pour réussir cette liquidation, Robbe-Grillet qui affirme que "le réel commence là où le sens vacille", crée un brouillage, un état de confusion qui prépare le lecteur-spectateur à entrer dans le nouveau système, à se soumettre à de nouvelles lois, à accepter d'autres principes d'organisation.

5. Il sera évident que le travail littéraire et cinématographique de Robbe-Grillet est en rapport étroit avec les *codes* qui gouvernent la production et la réception en matière d'art. Il y a longtemps, quand on lui a demandé à quoi servait le *Nouveau Roman*, il a répondu: "Le Nouveau Roman sert à transformer l'homme". Plus tard, il a beau ironiser de ce *statement*, je crois qu'il y a toujours cru, secrètement, avec ténacité, sans faire de concessions. Sa pratique de l'enseignement hors de France et ses multiples pérignations à travers le monde l'ont sans doute soutenu dans sa tâche de "transformateur". Car les codes ne sont pas universels: il sont géographiquement et culturellement déterminés et sujets à des changements. J'ai souvent dû constater que la place de Robbe-Grillet en France est problématique, sans doute parce que le code littéraire, inculqué par un enseignement national uniforme et sauvegardé par des institutions bien établies, s'y oppose au renouveau. C'est ce qui explique la forte présence du discours polémique dans les "Romanesques". Dans *Angélique*, par exemple, l'auteur, s'attaquant aux habitudes bien ancrées des lecteurs conformistes, déclare dans un métadiscours parfois très aggressif, qu'en proposant un "anti-texte", un discours fondé sur un "ordre autre", il offre au lecteur un autre monde possible, un "anti-monde". Il combat aussi bien "l'illusion réaliste" procurée par le discours de fiction traditionnel que "l'exigence de signification" contenue dans le discours du réel. Le mimesis étant impossible, il faut créer une nouvelle réalité, celle du *texte* - ou du film modelé selon les principes d'un autre ordre. Grâce à son exemplarité, ce texte ou ce film peut alors effectuer les transformations souhaitées chez le lecteur ou le spectateur. On a longtemps cru que l'homme a fait la langue. En réalité, mieux vaut dire que la langue fait l'homme. En transformant sa langue, on transforme l'homme. Chez Robbe-Grillet, les moyens employés sont parfois si audacieux, nous l'avons constaté, qu'ils risquent de provoquer le refus chez le lecteur. Tant pis, s'exclame l'auteur d'*Angélique*, quand il s'agit d'imposer son ordre à lui, "le romancier a même le droit de *tuer* son lecteur"!

Quelle est la visée de ce combat? Les procédés que nous avons observés sont manifestement des armes redoutables servant à abolir systématiquement la cloison qui sépare la réalité (l'histoire de

In the Temple of Dreams

Robbe-Grillet dans *Angélique*, la pseudo-réalité du tournage du film dans *Trans-Europ-Express*) et la fiction (l'histoire de Corinthe, le récit d'Elias). La "morale" est simple: la réalité de l'imaginaire - de l'inventé et du rêve - est aussi "réelle" ou plus, que celle de la réalité objective. (Je renvoie ici aux études d'Anthony Fragola et de Roch Smith sur la parenté de Robbe-Grillet avec le Surréalisme et sur le fonctionnement des "générateurs" dans le processus de création). En faisant glisser les niveaux narratifs et les identités des personnages, le texte ou le film fait également trébucher le lecteur ou le spectateur. Cette déstabilisation a pour effet soit l'abandon (on "tue" alors son lecteur), soit un plaisir esthétique semblable au vertige ("l'enchantement"). Dans le dernier cas, le discours des mots ou des images peut faire "vaciller" l'interlocuteur perturbé, lui enlever ses certitudes et le mobiliser dans le sens de la libération de son imaginaire refoulé. Par leurs reprises bien calculées, les glissements nous conduisent alors à la confusion du réel quotidien et du fictif onirique et nous font accéder à cet univers nouveau où les images fusionnent. C'est dans cette procédure esthétique du brouillage que se reconnaît l'intentionnalité profonde de ces oeuvres, intentionnalité qui dépasse manifestement les domains de la seule esthétique.

7. "The Blue Villa"
Within the Temple of Dreams

Professor Anthony Fragola
(University of North Carolina, Greensboro)

In *For a New Novel* Robbe-Grillet indicates that a dream is the basic structural principle governing his films. The New Novelists, Robbe-Grillet asserts, were attracted to cinema because of the added dimension of a soundtrack - cinema's possibility of acting on two senses at once, the eye and the ear - finally in the sound as in the image the possibility of presenting with the appearance of incontestable objectivity what is also only dream or memory, in a word, what is only imagination. These references to dream and imagination, and their ontological significance, establish a structural principle governing *The Blue Villa*. Robbe-Grillet has always sought not to imitate an external reality, but to create an internal one. Robbe-Grillet does not transcribe a dream, but, like Bunuel, he attempts to construct the mechanism of a dream. Regardless of the view one takes on the significance, process and structure of dreams, in the individual and in art, Freud's interpretation of dreams is fundamental to our understanding. Freud's well-known theory of dreams as the expression of the *Geist*'s fulfillment of repressed desires, of infantile sexual desires, offers a rudimentary way of viewing *The Blue Villa* - and I would like to stress *rudimentary*.

In the Temple of Dreams

The film opens with images of the sea and village in juxtaposition with a voice-over narration by Edouard Nordmann, known as Nord, who speaks using script format - "Interior. Night." then initiates the action - "A sailor's accidental drowning", he says, "One spring night a child slips while playing on the rocks and vanishes down a deep hole". Soon, with the arrival of the Chief of Police we discover that the voice-over is part of a script, a work in progress, unfolding as Nord dictates on tape. This chosen form of expression is crucial. He is not a poet, nor a novelist, but a screenwriter, whose work utilizes the two elements of sounds and images that Robbe-Grillet observes both in cinema and in dreams.

For Freud, the meaning of dreams is hidden or latent, and can be made manifest only by the dreamwork of analysis. Using Freud's model, the spectator could speculate on the latent meaning of Nord's dreams. His script could be regarded as the process of his unconscious mind transforming his repressed sexual desires for his stepdaughter into a form that utilizes the two salient features of a dream - sounds and images. The results would be more a reflection on the viewer-analyst, than on Nord's inner world, for Nord cannot respond to our questions and to associations, and leaves us to discover the latent meanings of these images and sounds organized into a script. Freud's approach leads to another problem of deciphering dreams in the dream-structure of *The Blue Villa*. Freud believes that the meaning of connecting disparate dream-thoughts is through verbal expression and he asserts the necessity of altering the verbal forms of some obscure dream representations to create linkages. This method would be antithetical to Robbe-Grillet's repeated statement that sounds and images must speak for themselves. Freud's theory also presupposes that words can explain images, and it negates the integrity of the dream to express its own meaning.

Recent theories of dream meaning, such as those of Hobson, dispute Freud's theories, and suggest that what is latent for Freud is actually manifest; in essense, what we see, is what we get. Freud's theories of condensation, dramatization, displacement and symbolism are possible tools for interpreting *The Blue Villa*. As Roy Armes states, "Every explanation is one of interpretation".

Condensation could explain *The Blue Villa*'s dream structure of juxtaposing and integrating the contradictory worlds of the far east with the film's primary location, the isle of Hydra in the Mediterranean. Nord has recently fled South-East Asia with a stepdaughter, Santa, who later accuses him of murdering her mother and attempting to murder her. The condensation could be attributed to the guilt he carries with him and the fear of discovery and retribution.

In displacement, the smallest detail can be the most significant, especially in a dream of great confusion. One small but significant detail, is the picture of the Dutchman on his ship, an obvious reference to Wagner's *The Flying Dutchman*. At the opening of the first act of Harry Küpfer's interpretation of the opera, a painting of the Dutchman falls off the wall, initiating the drama. Throughout the opera, Senta clutches the painting, illustrating that symbolic correlation of her psychic disturbance and its centrality to the meaning of her existence. Thus the painting in *The Blue Villa*, through association with Wagner's work, has both a generative function and an ontological significance.

For this discussion, the most important of Freud's hypotheses is contained in his concept of a dream-structure. He says - "Its portions stand in the most manifold logical relations to one another. They represent foreground and background, conditions, digressions and illustrations, chains of evidence and kinds of argument. Each train of thought is invariably contradicted by it's counterpart." Nord offers first one version of the events in which Frank, played by Fred Ward, has killed a young heiress, Nord's daughter Santa, because he could not marry her. As the Dutchman sought to escape, a sudden storm arose, killing him. "No. That's not it" Nord says. "Revision. Exterior. Day." He then offers another version that closely parallels the legend of *The Flying Dutchman*. Thus, the initial structure is based on the pattern that Freud outlines.

Freud's theories of the universality of dream symbols serve as the basis for Jung's work of archetypes that allows for more fruitful examination of *The Blue Villa*. Freud acknowledged that dream symbolism extends far beyond dreams. It is not peculiar to dreams, but exercises a similar dominating influence on representation in fairy-tales, myths and legends, in jokes and in folklore. It enables us to trace the intimate connections between dreams and these later productions.

The use of legends in *The Blue Villa* is markedly stronger than in any of Robbe-Grillet's previous films. Robbe-Grillet states: "In *The Man Who Lies* the underlying myth on which the story is developed - resistance against the occupier - is merely a rather vague reference, a backdrop, whereas in *The Blue Villa* the Wagnerian legend of *The Flying Dutchman* pervades the film even before the credits and until the end, as a structural motif, firm and inevitable."

Consistent with Jung's theories, the legend of *The Flying Dutchman* can represent the collective unconscious of a civilization that also finds a form of representation in dreams. In Wagner's *Memoirs of Heinrich von Schnappelwalski*, the Dutchman and Senta become representatives of archetypal concepts and the settings sea and land, infinite and finite, become symbols of the opposite poles of curse and redemption. Clearly, *The Blue Villa* has one of its key structural principles, a legend, expressed as a dream archetype, but it comes into conflict with narratives that are in themselves conflictual.

Contrary to Freud, Berthold States suggests that dreams are not manifestations of repressed desires, but the former thought, most free from repression. States views dreaming as a mental activity that is not a copy of our existence, but a reconstruction of it, and therefore at its origin, the dream is a mechanism of distortion, that is, a mechanism that falsifies the experience we have lived through because it does not render it as a probable structure or faithful account of events. First States asserts "Dreams are essentially a process or organisation of experi-

In the Temple of Dreams

ences." Nord's increasingly anguished attempts to write a script can be regarded metaphorically as the dream process itself in which the dreamer/scriptwriter attempts to organize his chaotic experience into a unified structure. As a metaphor for dreaming, Nord's script - incoherent and irrational - is subject to the same failures, false starts, dead ends and errors in thought as in the waking mind. If a dream is the process of thought, paralleled in a metaphor of writing a script, then Nord's script fails as a coherent finished shooting script, but succeeds as a first draught. Like a dream, Nord's script is presented as the process of thought as it occurs and not as images assembled like a finished, edited film. This script functions as an indicator of the disintegration of his thought processes.

Returning to Robbe-Grillet's statement in *For a New Novel,* that cinema reflects what is essentially dream or memory, States provides another way of looking at the similarities between dream structures and *The Blue Villa*. "In art, as in dreams", he says, "we process the patterns and qualities of life, never in its precise context, memory being less like a computer, than it is like a metaphor, that is, a kind of orderly mistake." Driven to despair, this would-be screenwriter, whose mind has been demented by attacks of fever, adulterated alcohol, memories, hallucinations and conflicting narrations impinging on him, Nord ultimately fails to create a coherent script. Essentially, the dream structure of *The Blue Villa* is one of competing realities that are resolved through the myth of *The Flying Dutchman*. "When dialectic fails to solve a problem, we resort to the mythical", says Robbe-Grillet, which Kierkegaard says, "is addressed not to the understanding, but to the imagination".

States' concept of scripts and archetypes provides additional insights into the structural form of *The Blue Villa*. In *Dream and Story-telling*, States notes that both fiction and dreams are usually narrated in form. Freud based his theories of dreams on the concept that dreams are a true manifestation of the dreamer's unresolved conflicts. Instead, States asserts, scripts created by the dream are not about the dreamer's problems, but problems are used to create narratives. In States' view, autobiographical content in dream and fiction is used for story construction, characterization, theme, and so on. Dreams are archetypes in terms of form and structural principle. Therefore, the viewer should not immediately assume, because of the contradiction between Nord's voice-over and images juxtaposed to it, that Nord's story is a fabrication of the truth, that he constructs solely to exonerate himself. Whatever alterations Nord makes to the events of his prior life, that are unknown, unverifiable and hence meaningless, he does it for the sake of the perfection of the plot. Or we can say that like dreams, Nord's story is fiction, but it is also true. As fiction that parallels the dream process, the story has its own integrity, its own truth, just as the contradictory narratives contain their own truths.

States' concept of the parallels between fiction and the dream process as embodied in archetypes, provides a useful frame of reference for *The Blue Villa*. For States, archetypes are omnipresent constructs, derived from the empirical world. Indeed, it would be impossible to write a meaningful fiction, or dream a dream that did not somehow lean on an archetypal model as its organising principle, since the principle of archetype is simply a special reference to the tensions arising from the value-structure itself. Since Nord is writing a script, the definition of a script is essential in establishing the relationship between Nord's story and the general structure of dreams. Scripts, for States, are memory structures of repeated experience that are capable of self-modification, and can be utilized in another context. Stories and fictions might be thought of as ways of sharing knowledge structures, dreams as ways of organizing private knowledge structures. States' insistence on the repetitive nature of scripts helps to explain not only Nord's obsessions, but the repetitions and obsessions that characterize all of Robbe-Grillet's films. *The Blue Villa* is a continuation of the dream structure that Robbe-Grillet established ever since *Last Year at Marienbad*.

Nord's script is in conflict with scripts dictated by what society regards as the ideal relationship between father and daughter. The Chief of Police confiscates Nord's script and dictates his own. The Dutchman arrives and challenges the events of Nord's script. Santa's real father writes his own narrative that eventually subsumes all others, especially Nord's. This structure of *The Blue Villa* is consistent with the parallel nature of dreams and fiction.

Dreams and fiction tend to be about the wages of getting out of step with the scripted world, of different interpretations of the same script, or a collision of personal goals with established scripts. For every script there arises the possibility of an anti-script. At the very outset of the film, Nord invites the Chief of Police to suggest an alternative ending.

This basic structural principle for both fiction and dreams functions much in the same way as Eisenstein's theory of montage, based on the theories of thesis and antithesis, a theory that also serves as Robbe-Grillet's method of shock in narrative construction. Thus, Robbe-Grillet's method of montage, first advanced by Eisenstein, parallels basic dream structure, just as Nord's attempts to write a script are similar to the dream process. This dialectic between order and disorder is the basic structural principle not only for *The Blue Villa* but for Robbe-Grillet's other films. "Order! Disorder!" bellows the magistrate who is surrounded by conflicting narratives in *The Progressive Slidings Towards Pleasure*. The dialectical nature found in dreams is mirrored in the duality between text and image. As Robbe-Grillet states - "The work that contains both an image and a text is going to be not an illustrated text, but an ensemble of contradictions in which the text and image are going to play antagonistic roles."

In *The Blue Villa* an immediate discrepancy exists between what is narrated off-screen in the voice-over narration, the text and the image. Nord's voice-over narration tells of the Blue Villa, a shabby brothel, while the viewer sees a splendid estate. The script

In the Temple of Dreams

speaks of landlocked sailors with their colonial malaria, while no sailors are seen, and the location is obviously a small island. Text and image thus create a dialectic that also parallels the opposition of the narrative and the struggle within it with the archetype. Archetypes are formed when scripts converge into archetypal patterns, repeated sequences of actions, and provide dreams and fictions with blocks of structure that can be joined or violated in endless ways. The structure of *The Blue Villa* is based on a dialectical pattern, not only between the conflicting narratives concerning death or the attempted murder of Santa, but of the narratives in conflict with the archetypal story of *The Flying Dutchman*, in which Senta, who roughly corresponds to *The Blue Villa*'s Santa, is herself a character scripted in an archetypal pattern of conflict with the norms of society.

Unlike Freud, who believed in the need to break down the structure of a dream into its individual parts, States calls for a need to examine the overall pattern, the '*Gestalt*' of the narrative, as a means to describe the brain's attempt to organize and thereby comprehend experience. In order to discern the truth, the meaning of the overall pattern of *The Blue Villa*, we must examine the relationship between Nord's dreams, his death, and the meaning of his existence. In Foucault's discussion of Binswanger's *Dream and Existence*, he seeks - "fundamental features of human existence, not in perception, but in the dream." Foucault's concept of the multiple possibilities of dream interpretation, of contradicting scripts, parallels that of States.

For both States and Foucault, dreams are not solely an expression of latent meanings. The dream is a fundamental composite, and if the meaning is invested in images, this is by way of a surplus, a multiplication of meanings which override and contradict each other. Foucault notes that Freud extrapolates only one meaning among many possible meanings and that Freud's psychological determinism reduces the potential richness of dreams. *The Blue Villa* creates a unified world, a *Gestalt* of paradoxical spaces, similar to the mechanism of a dream. Robbe-Grillet's comments about *Eden and After* also apply to *The Blue Villa*. As Robbe-Grillet notes, "The experience we have from life of these paradoxical spaces are times we also have in our dreams. You may have noticed that it is really impossible to narrate a dream. Besides, it is one of those things which caused Freud to flounder, because to narrate a dream is to replace within a rational system that which escapes rationality. I think that all of the relations to dreams that you have in the *New Novel* or in this type of film, are not there by accident, because this type of relation, this type of space, we have indeed within us."

Nord, the would-be screenwriter of the principal narrative (that others contradict, emendate, or attempt to control) seeks to impose a formal organized structure from paradoxical spaces - the far east with its game of Mah-Jongg and its players, the Asian ship, the Asian market, the rickshaw with its clacking wheels that echoes the incessant noise that drives men to madness, the market wares paraded by women juxtaposed to the world of the Mediterranean. Nord is trying to accomplish the impossible, to impose a rational order through the use of language that originates not from outside us, rather from within. In Nord's attempt to reconcile this contradiction, his script is doomed to failure.

Robbe-Grillet believes that artistic creation has to do with the imaginary, not with the real. Speaking of *Eden and After*, Robbe-Grillet offers insights into *The Blue Villa* - "In short, the materials that constitute the work of art are the stereotypes of a collective unconscious." Robbe-Grillet then quotes Descartes, who states - "*If I have dreamt of something with sufficient force, I do not know the next day when I wake up, whether it was real or not.*" Nord's anguished imaginings have taken on a reality in the intensity of a dream. He can no longer distinguish between what is external and internal. In essence, all is internal, as in a dream.

For Robbe-Grillet, one of the salient characteristics of man is that life is rooted in the imaginary. Extending this concept, Foucault believes that dreams are the basis for the imaginary, and not the imaginary the basis for dreams. Nord is a writer who seeks to bring into being the reality of his own existence. As Robbe-Grillet states when speaking of *The Man Who Lies* - "The writer is then the image of a man in general, an image at its most extreme of man, the inventor of his own life. In a way it is what Sartre has called freedom. The freedom of man is his ability to constantly invent the world." It seems to me that this makes for a beautiful conclusion. By inventing his own life through the imagination, Nord achieves a freedom that is foretold in the image of death found in the dreams. Foucault posits that the ultimate form of freedom is death as it is revealed in the dream. Nord's writing of a script, then, can be regarded as a metaphorical dream process that leads to ultimate freedom. Though at first it may seem that Robbe-Grillet and Dimitri De Clercq provide a happy ending, Robbe-Grillet cautions the audience not to forget to "identify less with the two reconciled lovers and more with this would-be screenwriter who is driven from his own text."

"*No. That's not it. Revision.*" In the spirit of Foucault, who criticizes Freud for seeking to extract only one meaning from dreams, another possible dream interpretation for *The Blue Villa* is offered. In Borges' story *The Circular Rooms*, the obligation of the central character is to dream a man into being. As in *The Circular Rooms*, Nord's anguished state can be regarded as the artist's struggle with the material, the manifestation of the psychic and creative energy required to fashion a work of art or a dream. He realized, in the story, that the effort to model the inchoate and vertiginous stuff of which dreams are made, is the most arduous task a man can undertake. As in *The Blue Villa*, Borges' story underscores the dialectical nature of dreams when they are in the incipient and most chaotic state. Just as in *The Blue Villa*, the ending of *The Circular Rooms* is abrupt, when, "in the dream of the man who was dreaming, the dreamt man awoke." Borges, who introduces the character of another off-screen dreamer, who directs the events of the narrative, finds another parallel struc-

In the Temple of Dreams

ture in *The Blue Villa*. Haunted by the spectres of his waking dreams, dispossessed, driven from his house, and above all his text - which equates to his life and the meaning of his existence - Nord sees his only recourse in death and the final absolution of the sea. In a moment of clarity, Nord foresees his death, not as the negation of his being, but the ultimate act of imagining, which Foucault believes is the expression of a dream. "Dream", he says, "does not point to an archaic image of phantasm or hereditary myth as its constituting elements. On the contrary, every act of imagining points implicitly to a dream. The dream is not the modality of the imagination, the dream is the first condition of its being." Returning to this primal source of his text - an expression of the imagination through the dream in which Santa appears to him and accuses him of her murder and infanticide - Nord foresees his final destiny, the death by sea, Robbe-Grillet's symbol of memory that awaits him.

In another hallucinatory sequence, Nord boards a rickshaw that exists only in his imagination to escape the Greek island. Conforming to an inner logic, dreams are steeped in the feelings that give rise to the images, thus when Nord boards a Rickshaw and tries to escape, the action and images capture his terror in entrapment. The frightening clatter of its wheels against the cobble-stones, as seen in vision by Dimitri De Clercq, immediately reminded Robbe-Grillet of the sounds of the Cart of Ancune in Breton Legend. Thus, a collective unconscious, not of images, but of sound. In his flight, Nord has not yet recognized Foucault's tenet that death can be seen as fulfilment and release - "No longer of a life interrupted, but the fulfilment of existence showing forth in the moment in which life reaches its fullness in a world about to close in."

"Exterior. The Dock. Night. The time of dreams and terror." The Dutchman looks down upon Nord floating in the sea, but the audience is never sure that he isn't just a figment of Nord's imagination, a creation of his dreams. "Exterior. Rocky Shore. Day. A fisherman holds Nord's body floating in peace as the Dutchman's ship passes with the Dutchman and Santa embracing." This is the new script's ending, dictated by Santa's alleged father, who has emerged so late in the narrative as to appear non-integrated and abrupt. The ending of Santa's father is appropriated from the ending of *The Flying Dutchman*.

It would appear, then, that the archetype has triumphed in the dialectic with conflicting narrations, but this, as Nord's expression of contentment indicates, is illusory. Nord's expression of contentment may mean that he has come to Foucault's realization that death is the ultimate freedom, the ultimate expression of the imagination which has derived from dreams, and that the meaning of his life, as in another Borges' story *The Secret Miracle*, has been fulfilled once this text is written. Nord's text is not his script, but his life that has come into its full being, and in his dream of death, a dream that he has staged in his drama, Nord "encounters what he is and what he will be, what he has done, and what he is going to do, discovering there the knot that ties his dreams to the necessity of the world." - Foucault's

In the Temple of Dreams

words appear to be the basis of the screenplay for *The Blue Villa*, as though he had foretold the future in a dream, or perhaps more pragmatically, Robbe-Grillet has appropriated them.

At the conclusion of the film a voice-over of Santa's father intones - "And so perished Edouard Nordmann, one Nord, without completing his alleged screenplay, without comprehending the tangle of knots which he himself had tied." As Dimitri De Clercq suggests, Nord's enigmatic look of tranquillity as he floats in the sea - perhaps in a sea of memory - belies the pronouncement of Santa's alleged father. Possibly Nord has recognized, just as the wizard of dreaming in Borges' story, that someone else was dreaming him. His mission accomplished, his text complete, Nord can relish the ultimate freedom as his being becomes one with the world. Through sounds and images, a dialectic between archetypes and conflicting narrations, Alain Robbe-Grillet and Dimitri De Clercq have given new meaning to Shakespeare's own text - "*We are such stuff as dreams are made on.*"

8. Sado-erotic Surfaces:
The 'Real' and the 'Represented' in "Nouvelles Autobiographies"

Professor Raylene Ramsay
(University of Auckland, New Zealand)

In August and September of 1996, the funerals of four young girls in Belgium put a whole country into a state of shock and mourning for young lives lost to the unthinkable. It appeared possible that their rape, humiliation, and perhaps even their death, had been filmed for a profitable paedophile video network. There was little doubt, as the first international conference on the sexual exploitation of children took place in Sweden, that a real if underground social reality was being represented.

The public reaction against the possible complicity in high places and the demand for greater measures for the protection of children required political responses. In France, for example, the leader of the Left-wing Socialist Party, Lionel Jospin, interviewed on recent world events on French television, recommended the toughening of laws for sex-offenders, and, why not, of the laws on pornography.

The slide effected here from repression of sadistic acts - of socially and morally unacceptable sexual violence against non-consenting human beings - to the necessity of censorship of all "deviant" representations of the "real" or the "imagined" is a common one. A few more thoughtful journalists observed that the only public access we have to the phenomenon outside crime reporting is through aestheticized representations, of a Lewis Carroll, an André Gide, the artist Balthus, for example. These literary and artistic works themselves become suspect: the nature of the relation between the literary and distanced representations and the desire of the writer (and the reader) is not evident. However, as Simone de Beauvoir answered her own question *Faut-il bruler Sade?* ("Should Sade be burned?") social science research and society too have generally concluded that rapists do not read Sade.

Filming or writing the various traces of the events in Belgium, the popular media constructed a story with all the elements of the sexual psycho-drama: the monster Mark Dutrou, in league with the Mafia, victims, eight year-old Julie and Melissa who were indeed purity and innocence incarnated, sequestration, torture and death, corrupt policemen, international conspiracy and sex-slave traffic. The mode of telling was linear, causal, coherent, that of traditional realism. Derrida argues that we are always within representation, within constructions, effects of truth. This may be so, but it seems evident that, in this case, there are "degrees of reality". to use an expression of Barthes. Despite the feedback loops between real sexual crime and its representations, that is, the circulation that makes events visible only through narrative, there is also difference.

These real events as told by the media are, however, curiously similar to the elements of the excessive fictions that proliferate and recur in Robbe-Grillet's "*New Autobiographies*". These autofictions are, it is claimed, a dance on the ruins of earlier characters and texts, of popular mythologies, and pseudo-confessions, a non-realist production of a "folie fabulante". In *Les Derniers Jours de Corinthe*, for example, there are fragmented stories of wild adolescent gangs sexually enslaving and punishing their more beautiful captives in a conflict to the death with an army more brutal even than the adolescents. The soldiers intern their adolescent prisoners in the old Lyric Theatre as an outlet for the hidden criminal desires of the authorities; austere magistrates, police, archbishops. In a scene based on what could be called the Herod-Salome complex, Corinthe is interrogated by the Professor of Parapsychology, Van der Reeves ("des rêves"), uncertain whether this Professor of Dreams is a policeman under-cover or an alter ego and an accomplice in crime. Robbe-Grillet as narrator and as film-maker directing the camera is the ironic figure of the investigator criminal on his own track, much as Robert Mapplethorpe photographs himself as the devil incarnate.

The character from the film, *La Belle Captive*, father of the very young Marie-Ange, Van der Reeves now appears to be the manager of a very young call-girl, offering his seductive ball-throwing daughter to Corinthe for the latter's nefarious purposes. Another quixotic figure from *La Belle Captive*, the police inspector, also makes his way to this South American frontier between Uruguay and Brasilia to interrogate Corinthe-Herod-Robbe-Grillet, suspected of being "le

In the Temple of Dreams

monstre marin qui dévore les fillettes" ("the marine monster who devours little girls"). A similar complex of criminal investigators or detective criminal narrators reappear in the most recent Robbe-Grillet work, the film *Un Bruit Qui Rend Fou* (*A Maddening Noise/The Blue Villa*, 1996). The crime investigated involves the abuse and possible drowning of the very young, angelic and perverse, Santa. Perhaps murdered by the returning villain, Franck, perhaps sacrificed by her own father, Santa may also be an hysteric. In either event, the camera shows scenes of Santa, or perhaps of her returning phantom, held as a sexual captive in the Blue Villa.

Like this recent film and its making and unmaking of the theme of incestuous desire for the young and beautiful daughter, Robbe-Grillet's autobiographical trilogy is not a realist narrative, nor is it simply a demonstration of the "richness of popular fantasies", although both of these constitute a particular kind of surface in his work. The history of the emergence of the great writer from specific socio-historical contexts, the memories of "formative" life events, I have claimed, are present as the material of a deconstruction of the conventions of traditional autobiography and the exploration of the (im)possibility of writing History and the Self. Along with the debris of Western culture, the ruins of the life become the generators of multi-layered, polysemic, moving new architectures of the imagination. But although the boundary between lived experience and recounted tale, between the sincerity and real reference of Lejeune's autobiographical pact and the imaginary constructions of fiction is moving and indeterminate, there are degrees of truth and of illusion; shifting alignments of very different kinds of building material.

"Le réel réduit au réalisme, quelle misère" ("realism for the real, what poverty"), declared Robbe-Grillet in his preface to the illusionist, ludic, comic-book novel, *Chausse-Trappes*. The real here is seen to be impoverished in its translation by realism, but its existence is not denied. The material of Robbe-Grillet's three autofictions include the collective; mythologies (water nymphs), Breton legends ("les lavendeuses de nuit" or enchanting/enchanted fairy washerwoman), knightly romances and the medieval "matière de Bretagne", opera. His material is also derived from the personal, the stories told by his parents and memories of his childhood (the tales of near drowning and accounts of the dangerous sea). Into the collective material, Robbe-Grillet consistently injects a dose of sado-eroticism that appears to have a connection with the confession of his own sado-erotic sexual phantasies and predilection for very young girls. The water nymphs are imprisoned and the faery washerwomen have hung up blood-stained undergarments to dry in the moonlight. The stories of the recent history of Europe, particularly the Second World War and Robbe-Grillet's own complex uncomfortable relation with Nazi ideology create a similar loop between outer and inner, private and public. So also do his readings of formative novels and re-interpretations of his own earlier writing. His text creates a circulation of intertextual quotation and assemblage from literature, opera, painting and intratextual

In the Temple of Dreams

quotation from his own earlier work. It puts into play the stereotyped imagery of a rejected sado-erotic confrérie and Robbe-Grillet's own "autofictional" stories of the childhood china dolls he carried up to bed and punished, dolls that reappear, stained with blood, on a shelf in the film *Un Bruit Qui Rend Fou*. The categories do not remain discrete and stable, but inside and outside, I argue, are not completely indistinguishable; these surfaces can have different textures and effects. The "art" of the *New Autobiographies* lies precisely in the shifting alignments among such different surfaces and different kinds of generators, used with different effects.

In the films, it is the shock set up between the aesthetic female bodies degraded to stereotypes, and their subsequent reinvestment and reworking by a very particular and obsessive imaginary of compliant captivity, submission, and blood on white flesh that is the source of both audience intellectual pleasure and emotional disturbance. The decors of the real Greek island in *Un Bruit Qui Rend Fou* are reinvested by the images of the Blue Villa, and the phantasmatic sado-erotic Orient in a similar movement that can be felt both as emotionally and intellectually pleasurable and as perilous. The soundtrack moves the listener between the maddeningly grating or violent repeated sounds (breaking glass, Santa's scream, off-key opera singing, the noise of the Mah-Jongg counters as they strike the table) at the limit of the tolerable and the power of the narrative as it begins, once again, to tell, or record, the "true story". The seduction of the story is reinforced by the striking images.

Both the images and the sound-track offer the viewer-listener the satisfaction of recognizing the intertexts that are reassembled here to make a new story, drawing him/her into the game of flattened stereotypes of the erotic, exotic crime narrative. At the same time any resolution, any completion of understanding is denied. The stereotyped images of sex and violence, the aggressive sound-track, and the circularity also create discomfort for the spectator and the listener.

The ludic organization of these movements between seduction and aggressive distancing and the dance between private and public, along the reversible surfaces of the Möbius strip, does not permit a return to an origin, an original, or a lived real as opposed to a representation. In *Les Derniers Jours de Corinthe*, however, the writer claims to have seen one of the tableaux he uses, that is, the twelve young girls in stages of filmy white (un)dress for their first communion, in a real shop window in Franco's Spain. He is indicating the presence of unconscious sacrificial sexual symbolism in this very Catholic conservative regime but also giving his suspect mise-en-scène an outside alibi. In *Angélique, ou l'Enchantement*, the story of the young virgin drawn and quartered, but first delivered over to her executioner to be deflowered, freezes to a representation in a history book of practices of capital punishment in seventeenth century Turkey. Again, the outside "real" of history is presented as preceding and feeding into Robbe-Grillet's imaginary.

In the Temple of Dreams

Yet, the artifacts that circulate from one work to another to reconstitute the most common of the recurring symbolic complexes - the fascination and fear of the entwining seaweed-feminine hair and the sea as devouring vulva, the provocative siren, child-woman (innocent and perverse little girl) and the blood-stained high-heeled blue shoe on the seashore that signifies her penetration and destruction - have evident links with the accounts of personal "real" near drownings in childhood Brittany, or in Martinique in L*es Derniers Jours de Corinthe*. In fact, the story told by Robbe-Grillet to his editor Jérôme Lindon at the end of *Angélique ou l'Enchantement*, of his adolescent sexual initiation by the precocious adolescent Angèle to games of master and slave, the trauma of the blood of her deflowering, and her "accidental" drowning on the Léon coast, or again Robbe-Grillet's account of his relation with his childwife Catherine appear to designate these lived experiences as origin of the fantasies produced by his fictional "dream machines". Corinthe's confused heroic/villainous fictional adventures in Europe and South America are evidently related to Robbe-Grillet's rightwing, Germanophile past. But therein lies the Robbe-Grillet tale. The exact nature of this relation, the relation between cause and effect, remains undecideable.

Any account of the past is necessarily captured in the present. The intervening experiences, fictional explorations and the work of the imaginary, affected in their turn by the images on the contemporary walls of the city, feed into and modify this capture of the past by the present. The nature ot the pleasures and dangers of Robbe-Grillet's staging of sexually violent images or of his breaking down of the "limen" or line between the lived experience and the imaginative fiction, remains as undetermined as the origins and meanings of the representations he puts into play. The question of the dangers inherent in the breaking down of the separation between real and imagined, however, in my view, remains a real one.

In a debate published in 1995 that rehearses many of the old arguments for and against censorship, Christine Boutin, former conservative French Parliamentarian, and crusader for tougher censorship of sexual images that turn the body of the other into an object of pleasure, argued that, presented in public spaces and thereby imposed on the unwilling individual, these undignified images are unwanted and unwonted. Jean-Jacques Pauvert, editor of the work of Sade and of eighteenth century libertine novels ("that one reads with one hand only"), bases his argument against any censorship of expression on the private nature of books and films (no one is obliged to read them) and on the impossibility of one private person or group deciding for others, the public, what is pornographic and what is dignified. (His question is who gets to be the arbiter of community standards).

Social science work in the United States and Britain has generally concluded, with Pauvert, that there is a lack of any statistical link between sex offending and the consumption of "pornographic" representations (defined initially as explicitly sexual images without any redeeming social or aesthetic value and more recently as images associating sex with violence). In a study of "preposterous" excessive aggressive media violence, James Twitchell has argued that the serial images of apparently gratuitous destruction present "an uncorrupted view of the phantasy life of male adolescents and of their transition from individual and isolated sexuality to pairing and reproductive sexuality." (p.46). His thesis of the cathartic function played by popular culture in its mythologizing of aggression is not one of a purging of passions, a cleansing that arouses terror and pity in the Aristotelian sense. The rituals of violence, claims Twitchell, "excite, incite, becalm, delay, and defuse aggression." (*Katharma*, before Aristotle, was synonymous with *pharmakon* in signifying at once poison and remedy). In France, in September 1996, in the wake of the manslaughter of a fifteen year old Marseille youth by a knife-wielding delinquent and the death of a high-school student shot accidentally in a skirmish with a school friend, a directive was issued by the Minister, Francois Bayrou, asking that programs including gratuitous violence not be shown at peak viewing hours. The mainstream, it seems, is reluctant to subscribe to such an anticommon-sense thesis and supports the opposing theory of modelling, that argues for the formative role of the images around us.

Robbe-Grillet has used both arguments: the catharsis argument to justify the presence of the sexually violent tableaux in his work; the formative role of the images on the walls of the city as an argument for our need to look with open eyes at the monsters concealed in these images. In their debate, both Boutin and Pauvert agreed, however, that public images or representations of real abuse and cruelty as in the case in paedophile video networks or so-called snuff movies, pose an extreme and unacceptable limit.

Yet, as Robbe-Grillet's autofictions have demonstrated, this boundary between real and simulacrum, public and private, is not quite as stable as it seems. Robbe-Grillet wrote the text of *Temple aux Miroirs*, for example, to accompany Irina Ionesco's photographs of her own adolescent daughter adorned only with the boas, roses, fur and pearls of "seduction". *The Temple of Mirrors* is a product of Irina Ionesco's images as they speak to Robbe-Grillet's *imaginaire*. It is also a conscious intertextual game of integration of this material from the temple of dreams with other stereotypes of the erotic from earlier Robbe-Grillet texts. The real was nonetheless sufficiently present in this particular surface of the Temple, in the form of the real body of a young woman who was still a minor, for the Brigade des Moeurs ("Vice Squad") to have requested the presence of the writer for questioning.

I have argued elsewhere that Marie-Ange, Angélique, Violette, Manrica, Temple, as you like her, is a skeptical staging and deconstruction of Western myths of the feminine (outside) but also a perverse game with Robbe-Grillet's own phantasies and his own lived relation to women as he confesses/conceals this, particularly, in his injection of the sado-erotic into medieval chivalry in *Angélique ou*

In the Temple of Dreams

l'Enchantement. The fair Angélique is not only enchantment, she is danger, her elf-like ethereal seduction must be resisted by her capture, imprisonment and pleasurable destruction. The spell she might cast on the male (who, of course, has a greater social investment in difference than the female) is that of sameness, non-differentiation: she would suck the unwary traveller or sailor down into the original depths, the salt-womb to drown. Corinthe, avatar of the narrator, resists self-loss in this feminine other by becoming himself the marine monster. This is the reading Robbe-Grillet gives of Ingres' representation of the myth of the chained Andromeda, delivered from the approaching sea monster by Perseus in *Roger délivrant Angélique*. For Robbe-Grillet, the sea monster is also the hidden face of Perseus. In the magic mirror that Corinthe drags out of the sea in *Le Miroir Qui Revient*, he catches a glimpse of his reproachful drowned fiancee, Marie-Ange. In the same recurring mirror, the rearing white horse (symbol of virility) sees his own death. The drowning of the feminine body is simply a self-protection from this threat. Through other destructions of the feminine body, quartered (the story of the young non-virgin bride of Tunisia), or tied to the tail of the station and dragged radiant through the ardent forest (the legendary Brunhilde), devoured by dogs and eaten (Boccaccio), penetrated by the sword (Delacroix's *La Mort de Sardanaple*) or drowned (Robbe-Grillet's Marie-Ange), the male separates from the all powerful or castrating or disappointing but still (spell)-binding mother. Robbe-Grillet's work casts an insistently bright light on this blind spot in our Oedipal culture and in his own life.

Salman Rushdie's figures of simulacra, for example the prostitutes that take on the names of the wives of the prophet, in *The Satanic Verses*, are post-modern creations for a sophisticated reading public. But these ironic and playful deconstructions are also a result of Rushdie's own hybrid educational and cultural experience. His disturbance of the Law remains within the law with which he takes personal issue; at every level, it is a provocation. There is also a question of reading. For those who have not learned to decrypt deconstructive texts (and most of those who condemn Rushdie did not read his novel), the text can only be blasphemous.

Robbe-Grillet's texts, too, are both deconstructions and a product of his own specific lived socio-historical contexts. They are a post-modern writing on the ruins, with humour, even verve ("nous écrivons désormais, joyeux, sur des ruines" he writes as his prologue to *Les Derniers Jours de Corinthe*). This does not prevent "his imagination speaking of memory", as he expresses it. His personal ghosts, appearing and disappearing in the distortions of the "returning" mirror, bear the marks of the fear of decomposition and loss of virility of Robbe-Grillet's own specific *corps-a-corps* with the law. Through what has been seen as the critical deconstruction of the autobiographical narrative with fictional narrative, Robbe-Grillet's autofictions break down the artificial line between past and present, history and story, self and self recounted by the other. For those who read

In the Temple of Dreams

traditionally, thematically, who see stories as pure memory or mimesis, these texts are pornographic or antifeminist. A postmodern reading of the new autobiographies, on the other hand, could claim that these texts are feminist, a liberation through a subversive staging of the cultural myths and popular representations (detective stories, thrillers, even religious symbolism) that systematically juxtapose sex and violence and thereby endorse the prevalence in our culture of violence against the feminine. My own reading would see this ritualized staging as both an exposing of and a certain complicity with the functioning of these images.

Defenders of these new texts against the reproach of sexism have pitched their arguments both at the level of the thematics - the female characters are more fascinating, lively, and always come out on top in the battle of the sexes and at the level of the structures. These representations are the impoverished popular stereotypes on the walls of the city unmade by Robbe-Grillet's new and mobile architectures. They are subversive textual bodies, not sexual bodies. Neither response appears to explain the particular choices among the ready-made material, the density of the sado-masochist complex.

A comparison between an account of a "lived" experience of sadomasochism and the material of Robbe-Grillet's erotic dreams establishes interesting parallels and provides a frame that makes certain of his characters and scenarios more comprehensible. In a 1995 interview on her experience of the sado-masochistic world in France, published in the periodical *Krisis*, Christine D. situates the earliest indications of her masochistic sexual preferences in the fascination exerted on her young imagination by stories of the burning of witches by the inquisition and the moral and sacrificial suffering of the early Christian martyrs, staples of Robbe-Grillet's texts. Christine is in good company - Duras' obsessive thematics of self-loss in the other, or the liquid poetics of a self-opening to penetration by the blade/tongue of God in Luce Irigaray's writing, or even the "*redoutable*" Simone de Beauvoir's early intense fascination with Christian martyrdom. An analysis of traditional popular romance fiction also reveals a central masochistic complex that consists of heroic passive feminine resistance to male brutality - as beauty tames the beast. Robbe-Grillet's work might be situated at the opposite pole - with the movie, *King Kong*, in which the last line claims "T'was Beauty killed the Beast". In contemporary culture, too, Madonna, Michael Jackson, an emerging sadomasochistic lesbian and homosexual literature, and practices such as piercing, tattooing, branding of the intimate parts of the body, join the traditional bondage magazines and sex-shop materials as evidence of interest in these traditionally underground sexual representations and practices.

Christine D. discovered her sexual nature as sadomasochistic from her first meeting with her future husband, whom she presents as a strong initiator (one thinks of Duchemin, the handsome exotic stranger in *L'Eden et Après* who will initiate the compliant Violette into a similar liberation of her sexual nature). Christine D. describes sado-masochism as a game with specific rituals marked by theatralization and presents it as a refined and cerebral libertine erotic practice. This could constitute a partial description of Robbe-Grillet's texts. These rituals create pleasure, she claims, not simply through pain, but rather through the consent of one partner to accept humiliation, to submit totally to a master who controls the game in a relationship of absolute trust.

The victims in Robbe-Grillet's theatrical scenarios are all portrayed as consenting, complicitous, even transfigured, as cries of pain and cries of pleasure become indistinguishable. I would suggest that this description could be extended to the relation between the narrator and his "ideal" reader or spectator in Robbe-Grillet's work.

Women in the sado-masochistic confrérie are generally bisexual, according to Christine D. They are able to change roles from slave to mistress to please the master. Men usually lack such versatility. In Robbe-Grillet's work which stages such all-female exhibitionist scenarios in *L'Homme Qui Ment* and *Un Bruit Qui Rend Fou*, I argue, the narrator almost never takes the point of view of the humiliated victim and remains fairly safely at the pole of voyeuristic control even although, in a reversal characteristic in psychoanalytic literature, he stages scenarios in which the cruel persecutor sees himself as the victim, and the fair victim as cruel temptress; scenarios in which the victim assumes the guilt of her "just" punishment.

The stereotypes in Robbe-Grillet are not taken randomly from the walls of the city. A particular position of desire is at work in the films, for example, in the blindfolds, bent head exposing the nape of the neck, chopping block, accessories in the sexual games of mistress and slave among women observed voyeuristically by the eye of the camera in *L'Homme Qui Ment*. In *Un Bruit Qui Rend Fou*, Sarah la blonde, the Madam of the Blue Villa, an establishment for clients with special tastes, will play out sado-erotic scenes with her young 'pupil', Santa, threatening her with punishment. She, too, is watched by a camera eye situated at the sadistic pole. The bondage magazine read by Trintignant in *Trans-Europ-Express* which shows a naked girl tied to a railway track or the apparently gratuitous scenes of Eva consenting to be tied to the bedpost and raped (murdered?) to the grand airs of Verdi are also representations of women's bodies for a camera eye that is not neutral. Violette's initiation into sado-masochism by the handsome macho stranger in *L'Eden et Après* is certainly not one of female sexual liberation (as Robbe-Grillet has claimed) in any common understanding of that expression although the camera follows her more obsessively than Duchemin. Only women's bodies are exposed, undressed, and punished. The watching eye appears to be a masculine one.

In arguing that Robbe-Grillet, as 'subversive' writer/narrator or filmmaker, remains voyeuristically at the pole of 'masculine' control, thereby showing a lesser versatility than the women in Christine D.'s universe, who are able to move from the pole of dominated to that of domination, from "feminine" to "masculine", I note that other subversive contemporary male artists have not always sought the same control. Robert Mapplethorpe's powerfully artistic and sexually transgressive photographs stage both male and female bodies, and present sado-erotic scenarios in which the meanings of masculine and feminine slide and become multiple, in the face, for example, of a transvestite or chained masochistic Mapplethorpe, or a woman bodybuilder. This breaking down of the masculine-feminine dichotomy to produce gender fluidity and multiple sexual identities is not present in Robbe-Grillet's work, which, paradoxically, continues to stage scenarios close to Balzac's nineteenth century observation that "la femme est une esclave qu'il faut mettre sur un trône" (Woman is a slave who must be placed on a throne).

Like Robbe-Grillet, Christine D. is unable to find any unconvincing single origin for her sexual preferences or for the very particular character of the representations that capture her body and mind (Barthes' "*punctum*"). Along with the psychoanalytic theory of the sado-masochistic structure of the psyche (a struggle for domination between the ego and the super-ego), a theory of repression would seem to provide the most convincing explanation of the elitist and cerebral aspect of the practice. Christine D. states that sado-masochism exists mainly in North America, Northern Europe and Japan, that is, in undemonstrative non-Latin countries not touched by the more extroverted Catholic traditions of confession, nor indeed by the dolorism of Catholic iconography. For her, the flagellated, pierced, bleeding martyred modern Christ who replaced the stoic sage of Romanesque art serves a cathartic purpose. In a more egalitarian society, imbalance of power can be experienced vicariously by a shared mise-en-scène of domination and submission in which one partner upholds separate selfhood and rationality while the other shares vicariously in the self-dissolution, the transgression of the limits of the self experienced by the other.

I would argue that looking with open eyes at the monsters in society and in ourselves, at the link between our lives and our representations (which is which?) is still a central project in Robbe-Grillet's *Romanesques* (or "*New Autobiographies*"). And if we look hard at the phantasy of the immobilized (fettered), silenced (gagged) beautiful captive, Angélique, guardian angel and sacrificial victim, before it dissolves into the cloud formations above the temple of dreams, it is evident that she brings together some very old fears of woman's dual nature. Woman has indeed always been seen as "enchantment" - enchanting and enchantment, pleasure and danger. Her second face (Robbe-Grillet's Vanadé, *vaincu/victorieuse*) that of the dominating, self-possessed Angel of Death, Vampire, Bordello Mistress, as you like it, makes Angélique secretly guilty of, and therefore complicitous in, her own cruel wounding. It can be argued that Robbe-Grillet's punished victim is always feminine because he is exposing to the reader's gaze the social gendering of the sado-masochistic relations of the psyche in the real world (the construction of gender as difference, masculine and feminine, active and passive, and of gender as hierarchy and power, the masculine dominating the feminine. This is a product in its turn of traditional symbolic representations of women as masochistic. Such a reading might permit this work to be considered at least partially "feminist" (that is, acknowledging the deep roots of women's oppression and seeking to eradicate it by a transformation of society, or, in this case, of societies' representations). But it is also possible to argue that the return of the real/repressed in these autofictions, made invisible by the effacing of the boundaries between real and representation, derives from a particular and perverse masculine personal agenda; that there may be a certain pleasure or complicity in the representations of the capture, rape, and destruction of the feminine; her fixing at the pole of consenting victim. The reader, for her or his own part, rnay wish to resist a certain persuasion and desire to re-establish boundaries or degrees of reality, or to seek a theory of reference that recognizes differences among representations. S/he may wonder why the binary opposition of real and imaginary is deconstructed whereas the masculine/feminine dichotomy remains very traditional. Although women characters may be situated at the active and masculine pole of sadism and men at the pole of the feminine (the magistrate in *Glissements Progressifs du Plaisir*, the bleeding and drowned father in *Un Bruit Qui Rend Fou*, the father and indeed the child Alain in the *Romanesques*), the point of view of the narrator or of the camera, although constantly threatened, remains situated strongly in masculine control.

THE WRITER ON THE SCREEN

Speaking of the pleasures/dangers of the sado-masochistic universe, Christine D. claims that although there are implicit rules, signals to tell the other when to stop, to indicate one's limits, the excitement of the game is to attempt to draw the other always a little farther. In Robbe-Grillet's monstrous sea-stories, humour and distancing mechanisms notwithstanding, the real/realist reader, without very open eyes, may be the real victim. Robbe-Grillet has, as ever, forestalled me in these *Romanesques*, which openly threaten the reader with death - "*ta mort à toi, o lecteur*" ("Death to you, my reader") - sucked down by enchantment to drown, but in what depths?

---

9. The Mirror of Meta-Fiction:
Robbe-Grillet as the Writerly Reader of Trans-Europ-Express

Professor Royal S. Brown
(Queen's College, University of New York)

It is probably safe to say that all of the fictional works of Alain Robbe-Grillet are self-reflexive, whether his short stories, novels, films or even - and perhaps especially - his three recent forays into the field of autobiography, gathered together under the rubric *Romanesques*. Like M.C. Escher's hand drawing an identical hand, Robbe-Grillet's pen and his camera continually reveal to the reader-viewer the creative processes that produce acyclical, circular, contradictory and fantasy-laden structures that serve as narratives in his various works. But if there are degrees of self-reflexivity, then it is probably safe to say that it is his second film as a director, *Trans-Europ-Express*, first released thirty years ago, that stands as his *most* self-reflexive work. It is certainly his funniest. Consider, for instance, the fact that this is the only one of his films in which the author/cinéaste plays one of his own characters, and a major one at that (two years later he will have a small role as a press attaché in Alain Resnais' neglected *Je t'aime, je t'aime*, and Robbe-Grillet also appears very briefly in *L'Eden et Aprés* and *Glissements Progressifs du Plaisir*, though I would not really refer to these as 'roles'). Consider the fact that his character in *Trans-Europ-Express* is a filmmaker, who, aboard the Trans-Europ-Express between Paris and Antwerp, concocts, along with his continuity-person (which is how I am going to refer to what was very sexistly referred to back then as the "script-girl") and producer, an erotic thriller that parallels, interrupts, overlaps with and sometimes contradicts the erotic thriller starring Jean-Louis Trintignant and Marie-France Pisier that is the other half of *Trans- Europ-Express*. Consider also that the continuity person is played by Robbe-Grillet's wife, Catherine, who appears in all of the director's films through to *Glissements Progressifs du Plaisir*. This is also the only one of Robbe-Grillet's films to pull back and show the movie camera at work. This occurs some ten and a half minutes into the film, as the producer/ continuity person/writer-director triumvirate has just re-begun the story and Trintignant finds himself back at the railway station - Paris' Gare du Nord. For a moment we see a film crew, including Robbe-Grillet, backtracking a camera on a dolly. The film then cuts to Trintignant, seen, probably, in the backtracking shot whose making we have just witnessed.

But the self-reflexivity of *Trans-Europ-Express* does not just relate to the process of creation. It involves as well, and perhaps even more strongly, the psychology of the power struggle between the writer and the reader, between the filmmaker and the film-spectator. Typically in Robbe-Grillet, and especially in his films, we see male characters who either try to impose their stories on a woman or who try to clarify the mysteries of the woman's story. X, the man, spends most of *Last Year at Marienbad* trying to convince A, the woman, that "his story" is "history". The orphic hero of *The Immortal One* is relentless in his efforts to bring the secrets of his Eurydice, called "L", out of the darkness and into the light. In *The Man Who Lies*, Boris, also played by Jean-Louis Trintignant, spends the film telling different versions of *his* story to the film's various female characters, and also, rather meaningfully, to the audience. And it is in particular the role of women in Robbe-Grillet's work culminating in the characters of Violette in *Eden and After* and Alice in *Progressive Slidings towards Pleasure*, to resist what I will refer to as "rape" by the linear narrative, the type of narrative that the *Trans-Europ-Express*, running on an inexorably fixed line of tracks between Paris' Gare du Nord and Antwerp, could be said to symbolize. We should also keep in mind that a major part of Michel Fano's *partition sonore* (the sound score) for *Trans-Europ-Express* is made up of fragments from Verdi's opera *La Traviata*, in which Violetta, a courtesan, proclaims in the opera's most famous aria "Sempre Libera" ("Always Free"), that she lives for pleasure and for freedom. We in fact hear part of this aria during a scene where Trintignant, having bought some rope and chains, begins to get serious about his rape-bondage fantasies. But in *Trans-Europ-Express* these patterns of struggle tend to become much more complex. Robbe-Grillet has described this element of the film as follows, in an interview with François Jost. Having noted that the Trintignant character - whose very name Elias [Alias] implies the desire to avoid being pinned down by a name - consistently resists the role he has been assigned to play by the drug-smuggler, Robbe-Grillet goes on to note that:

"At a certain moment, furthermore, he (Trintignant) tells his story to a café-waiter as if he himself had become the narrator. And, if one pays careful attention, one notices that all the other characters, without exception, try at one moment or another to take control. *Trans-Europ-Express* is a battle, a battle for control of the narrative. The Producer: one perceives quite quickly that he is manipulating the author. It is he who establishes the directives and the principal axes of the story-line. The Continuity Person: she is the eternal watchdog; she is the bureaucracy that is also trying to take control in order to organize the story. Trintignant himself is also manipulated. Not only by the author but by Franck, the leader of the gang. One realizes that it is Franck who is organizing the entire story, is likewise being watched over by the Police Inspector, who in turn manipulates him. And the Prostitute (Marie-France Pisier): she shuffles the cards at each moment. She is at the heart of all these manipulations and she is constantly committing infractions of the rules, set up by each one of these narrators. She constantly upsets the story on one level, and throws it onto another level."

One might add to this that Jean-Louis Trintignant, alias Elias, also tries to create his own narrative vis-à-vis the prostitute (whose name is the generic Eva), playing out his rape fantasies, with him performing

In the Temple of Dreams

the role of the murderous rapist and her becoming the victim: "What do you like?" Eva asks Elias. "Rape", he answers, "Strictly rape". And it is here that we get to some of the deeper levels of meaning, implicit not only in the self-reflexivity of Robbe-Grillet's cinematic texts, but also in the controversial sado-erotic imagery that pervades both his novels (including his *Romanesques*) and his films. In just about all of Robbe-Grillet's fiction, cinematic or otherwise, there exists the possibility of a conventional narrative - a crime-drama, a love-triangle, a war story or whatever - which, in its closed-ended linearity and its causally motivated psychologies, would produce what, six years after the making of *Trans-Europ-Express*, Roland Barthes would refer to as the "*texte lisible*" - the "readerly text" - in *S/Z*, his brilliant essay on reader-liberation. For Roland Barthes, the reader of the "*texte lisible*" is a passive consumer of a product whose chief function is to be thrown away and replaced by a newly purchased product. For Robbe-Grillet, the producer of the "readerly text", which he fantasizes being, or resisting that urge with every fibre of his being, is nothing more than a rapist. We need go no further than *Last Year at Marienbad*, which climaxes in the apparent rape of "A", created by Alain Resnais' multiplied track-ins on the seemingly ecstatic heroine. And of course X, who has been trying throughout the film to force his version of history on A, immediately denies any unwholesome intentions: "*Non*", we hear in the voice-over narration, "*Ce n'était pas de force*" - No, it wasn't by force. In *Trans-Europ-Express*, Robbe-Grillet, as he notes in the interview with François Jost, fantasizes himself as the "stereotype of an author", or, perhaps it should be translated as the "stereotype of an auteur", an author who, one supposes, would be capable of producing a readerly text à la Balzac. Robbe-Grillet and/or his stereotypical author/auteur also fantasize a character alias Elias, who moves in parallel with the author/auteur and invents games of rape and murder with an Antwerp prostitute. Eva makes the fatal mistake of trying to take control of the drug-smuggling narrative in which Elias is trapped, which then gives him the excuse to make the fatal mistake of transgressing the limits of the rape fantasy-fiction he controls by "really" strangling Eva, thereby entering the domain of the readerly text, which supports, and is supported by, the patriarchal ideologies which have a vested interest in passing fiction off as history. For his error, Elias is set up by one super-ego figure, the Police Inspector, and shot down by another, Franck, the apparent head of the drug-smugglers.

Neither Robbe-Grillet nor his stereotypical author/auteur named Jean (the first part of Trintignant's double first name) makes this same fatal error. In order for the reader not to be raped by the linear narrative s/he must no longer be, as Barthes has put it, "a consumer but a producer of the text". Barthes describes this "ideal text" as follows (in *S/Z*):

"The systems are multiple and create interplays with each other, without any single one being able to dominate the others. This text is a galaxy of signifiers, not a structure of signifieds; it has no beginning; it is reversible; one can access it via various entries

In the Temple of Dreams

not one of which can be definitively declared to be the principle one; the codes that have mobilized us line up as far as the eye can see. They are indecideable (Their meaning is never submitted to the principle of decision, except by the throw of a dice); out of this absolutely plural text, systems of meaning can take over, but their number is never closed off since it is measured against the infinity of language."

Barthes might as well be describing *Trans-Europ-Express*. The film offers at least three narrative systems: (1) the attempts by the triumvirate to create a screenplay, (2) the drug-smuggling story which may be either an independent narrative, a series of amusingly stereotypical tests staged by Franck to test Elias or the screenplay in the process of being written, tape-recorded or filmed, (3) the relationship between Elias and Eva, which seems to be based almost entirely on play-acting.

These systems certainly interact with each other. The first act of RobbeGrillet's stereotypical author/auteur, for instance, is to look at a girly magazine at a newspaper stand in the Gare du Nord, which aligns him with Elias and his rape fantasies. Once the train has left the Gare du Nord, Elias enters the compartment where the film-maker, continuity person and producer, who will later identify him as Trintignant, are sitting. In a virtuoso piece of film-making, Robbe-Grillet uses editing, mirror-shots and apparent eye-line matches to suggest the contiguity, if not continuity, of the intersecting narrative systems. Even a pan from Catherine Robbe-Grillet to Trintignant never quite captures the two in the same frame. *Trans-*

Europ-Express certainly offers the possibility of multiple points of entry into its various narrative structures, which the visual language of the cinema is able to present as various places, such as the Paris Gare du Nord, the Antwerp railroad station, the waterfront, Eva's room and so forth. A graveyard for old railroad cars, however, seems to act as a kind of degree zero for these points of entry. In the interview with François Jost, Robbe-Grillet also notes that he set up patterns of reverse causality within the drug-smuggling narrative. Each of the tests undergone by Elias in the first part of the film actually lead him back to Paris, so that he can begin to smuggle cocaine "for real". There is even a moment in the film where a ringing bell heard faintly in Michel Fano's *partition sonore* (which is a kind of Musique Concrète) is interrupted when the inspector picks up a phone receiver.

Barthes, also, later on in *S/Z*, establishes certain parallels between musical and literary structure, suggesting that if the readerly text is close to the hierarchical patterns of tonal music then the writerly text has its closest equivalent in atonal music, and, I might add, in serial music, in which the individual elements of a particular series - in music the twelve notes of the chromatic scale or the instrumental timbres - is mobilized for a particular composition, exhausting itself in various permutational and combinational interactions rather than meeting quasi-causal ends in pre-ordained resolutions. Throughout his career Robbe-Grillet has applied serial devices to both his literature and his cinema, most transparently perhaps in his film *Eden and After*. In *Trans-Europ-*

In the Temple of Dreams

Express, as in the novel *The Maison de Rendez-Vous* - written one year earlier - serialization presents itself most obviously on the levels of story-telling and presentation. At one point or another during its one and a half hour length, *Trans-Europ-Express* offers the following possibilities of story-telling and/or fantasy generators, which, in their near inexhaustiveness, form one of the major series of the film:

(1) The movie itself, reinforced by the momentary revelation of the camera and crew at work.

(2) A kind of comic-script acting out of the story, complete with false beards and round bombs with fuses, seen before the title sequence.

(3) Opera. Fragments of Verdi's "La Traviata" punctuate the music track.

(4) A book or magazine. Three pieces of reading material - a book entitled *Transes*, with a picture of a train on the cover, a pornographic magazine entitled *Europe*, and the French news-magazine *L'Express* - spell out a punned version of the film's title.

(5) Scriptwriting.

(6) Tape-recorded narration.

(7) Oral narration, when Elias tells the café-waiter part of his own story in the third person singular. This particular persona created by Jean-Louis Trintignant seems to carry over into Robbe-Grillet's next film *The Man Who Lies*, (which the *Express* cover in fact foreshadows, since it announces the news story of

"*l'homme qui est mort quatre fois*" [the man who died four times], which is precisely how many times Trintignant's character Boris Varissa will die in *The Man Who Lies*.

(8) Play-acting. Seen in particular in the various exams the gang imposes on Elias and in his staging of the rape-fantasies.

(9) Poster-Art. Notably a poster for the James Bond movie *From Russia with Love* in the waiter's room.

(10) Comic books. In one of the comic books Elias has bought in Paris for the waiter in Antwerp, there is a comic-book rendering (panel) of a shot seen earlier in the film in which the Police Inspector is spying on Elias from a staircase in the Antwerp train station. In the comic-book the character replacing Elias is saying "*Mmm. Je crois qu'il m'a repéré!*" ("Mmm. I think he's spotted me.").

(11) Postcards.

(12) Newspaper stories.

(13) The strip-tease, used by the police inspector to trap Elias. We see a nude woman on a platform whose rotation causes the strip-teaseuse to be wrapped in a large chain, coming from off-stage.

And there are no doubt more. While Robbe-Grillet does not attach each of these modes of story-telling cells with other serial cells in the film in a quasi-Boulezian exhausting of the permutational-combinational possibilities, they work their way sufficiently

In the Temple of Dreams

into the filmic structure to create a sense of serialism in the reading of the film. As one example, Robbe-Grillet's voice creating the story occasionally shows up on the voice-tracks of scenes in which Elias is acting out the same story. The combination of the two momentarily creates the possibility of a third type of cinema, namely, the crime-drama with voice-over narration.

I could go on with ways in which Robbe-Grillet in *Trans-Europ-Express* has created the perfect cinematic equivalent of Barthes' *texte scriptible*, perhaps we could call it the *film tournable* - the "shootable" film! But it seems to me that *Trans-Europ-Express* raises an even bigger issue. It has never been clear to me whether Barthes, in *S/Z*, is suggesting that certain *texts* are writerly while others are readerly, or whether all artistic texts are potentially writerly, in which case whether the text is writerly or not depends wholly on how it is read rather than on how it is written. This would certainly seem to be borne out by the text chosen by Barthes for analysis in *S/Z*, a story entitled "Sarasine", by none other than Honoré de Balzac, the *capo di tutti cappi* on Robbe-Grillet's list of *bêtes noires* in the field of novel-writing. (For me, "Sarasine" is a perfect example of the unfairness of Robbe-Grillet's harsh attitudes toward Balzac.) With the above in mind, and remembering Barthes' earlier definition of the *texte scriptible* as one in which the reader is a *producer* of the text, it occurred to me on this particular coming-to-grips with *Trans-Europ-Express* that the character played by Robbe-Grillet in the film is not the writer but rather the reader of the filmic and other texts. As we have already seen, *Trans-Europ-Express* abounds in images of reading and story-telling. One is also reminded of a passage from Robbe-Grillet's 1957 novel *Jealousy* in which the female character and her possible lover, named Franck, are discussing a novel they have both read. Both invent new hypotheses for situations they have not found believable, leading to "other bifurcations . . . each one of which leads to a different ending. The variants are quite numerous, the variants of the variants even more so." In *Trans-Europ-Express* Elias reads a newspaper article, planted by a police inspector, telling of the murder of Eva. Beneath the article is an ad, also planted by the police inspector, for the striptease that I have described earlier. The juxtaposition of the two is a perfect visualization of the fantasy turned into quasi-historical reality that is the readerly text. Elias, by going to the stripshow, tries to return to the domain of fantasy as fantasy, but it is too late, and his punishment is inevitable and swift.

In the first of his three *Romanesques*, *Le Miroir Qui Revient*, Robbe-Grillet confesses that he never had children because he would have had no use for a boy, and because he most surely would have had a sexual liaison with a girl. One has the impression that the Author-Auteur is so constantly tempted to transgress the frontier between fantasy and reality that he has had to invent artificial constraints, such as not having children, to avoid it. In Robbe-Grillet's creative life, one has the similar impression that the Author-Auteur is so bent on avoiding rape by the text,

In the Temple of Dreams

that he actually takes control of both ends of its production, at least in his own texts. Robbe-Grillet's texts become writerly, not so much because of the freedom they give to the reader, but because the text becomes a writerly reading of itself. In so doing, the very text becomes a weapon against dominance and/or rape. One in fact has the right to wonder whether, in creating himself as the writerly reader Robbe-Grillet has not co-opted this position as a possibility in the potential readers of his films and novels, in other words, the possibility of a writerly reading of the text becomes impossible because Robbe-Grillet has basically pre-empted that possibility. *Trans-Europ-Express* offers a perfect image of the text as weapon in the book entitled *Transes* that I alluded to earlier. On the cover of this book is a train moving along on tracks, a perfect image, as I have already suggested, of the linear narrative. But when Elias opens the book, we discover that, after the first few pages, the rest of the book has been hollowed out and contains a gun. The whole image might just as well be called "The Reader Strikes Back". On an even more subliminal level, however, we may or may not notice that the pages that do remain in the book are from the French translation of British novelist Winston Graham's book *Marnie*, on which Alfred Hitchcock based his film *Marnie,* which appeared two years before *Trans-Europ-Express.* In his interviews with Anthony Fragola and Roch Smith, Robbe-Grillet refers to *Marnie* as "a particularly bad film encumbered with popular psychology". That may or may not be, and I personally do not agree with that judgement, but the allusion to the *Marnie* narrative certainly reinforces, intertextually, the theme of the fear of rape, both physical and textual. Marnie, played by Tippi Hedren in the film, subverts the domain of the father by taking on phoney names - aliases - getting jobs and then stealing her employer's money. She is caught by a man played appropriately enough by Sean Connery, who, like N. in *The Immortal One*, tries to reconstruct Marnie's story, in this case, by playing the grand-daddy of psychology and psychological causality, Sigmund Freud. Like many of Robbe-Grillet's heroines, Marnie's role is to resist this form of rape. At a moment when the Connery character is in Marnie's bedroom and is bombarding her with a classic round of psychological questions, Marnie taunts him with the line "You Freud, Me Jane." Undeterred, Connery has already married Marnie, knowing she is frigid, and on their honeymoon he promptly proceeds to rape her. In *Trans-Europ-Express* Robbe-Grillet amusingly offers as one of the possible explanations for the theft of Elias' book by a woman in glasses, that the woman was perhaps a kleptomaniac. This is precisely how Marnie is described through much of the novel and Hitchcock's film.

In Robbe-Grillet's mind at least, to allow the fictional text to fall into the Balzacian "illusion of reality" rather than stressing the reality of the illusion, is to transgress the Lacanian *loi du père* - the law of the father - just as severely as if he had committed rape or incest - or a tricky Oedipal combination of the two. And therefore the punishment for such a transgression would be just as inexorable and just as cruel as the one meted out on Elias near the end of *Trans-Europ-Express*. And so, the penultimate acts of the character played by Robbe-Grillet in the film are an act of reading and an act of refusal. Returning to Paris' Gare du Nord with his producer and continuity person, Robbe-Grillet picks up a newspaper and reads of both Eva's murder and Elias' assassination in Antwerp. The producer, of course, thinks this would be a great subject for a film. But Jean refuses, noting, in the film's final line of dialogue "*Avec la réalité, il y a toujours des ennuis*" - with reality you always have problems). Having thus, once more, eluded the system, Jean is now able to separate himself from the producer who needs a linear narrative to make money, and the continuity person who must maintain visual and narrative cohesion to keep her job. Moving off to the right, Jean is rewarded for his writerly correctness as he comes across Elias and Eva, who apparently aren't "really" dead after all, in a happy embrace. Or perhaps it is Jean-Louis Trintignant and Marie-France Pisier. Or it might even be Jean-Louis Trintignant as the hero of Claude Lelouch's 1965 *A Man and a Woman*, a film Robbe-Grillet no doubt thoroughly loathes, in a reprise of that film's final shot, but with Anouk Aimée replaced by Marie-France Pisier. With reality, you always have problems.

10. Open Discussion

Hosted by Ann Jefferson
(Lecturer at Oxford University)

Ann Jefferson: In the light of the last two papers, I think what Raylene was saying and what Royal was saying was to a certain extent similar, and that is that Robbe-Grillet has mastered the language of criticism that we all live by so effectively as to stitch up what we can do. And I wonder what the six of you here, in order to speak about Robbe-Grillet as critics, might have to say about that.

Royal Brown: I definitely agree. I think that it's a great ploy. It gets us all interpreting his texts, and at the same time interpretation is very much validated by his own hand and encouraged by his own hand. I mean to a certain degree it seems to me a very massive pre-emptive strike.

Raylene Ramsay: I think I would absolutely agree with Royal. I think I was trying to argue that there is space for critical reading.

Ben Stoltzfus: In a sense he's continuing his career dialogue with us, the critics, who have helped make his career. We live off him and he lives off us, and we all live happily in this symbiotic relationship with him which we share.

In the Temple of Dreams

Roch Smith: I think I would take issue with the notion that we are interpreters, however. Using Susan Sontag's notion against interpretation, I think Robbe-Grillet's kind of text, whether it is filmic or verbal, argues against meaning and interpretation - and for consideration of form, in particular in the narrative process. And we do that - whether we think we're doing it, or are aware that we're doing it - *we end up doing it*. However I don't think anybody today attempted to talk about meaning in Robbe-Grillet, really.

Royal Brown: The point that I would suggest is that we can do that with any text. The fact that Barthes can do it with Balzac means that any text, really, has all these possibilities in it, and that all of those possibilities of reading are built into Robbe-Grillet texts as a part of the text. So in other words it is, as I said, a mirror of meta-fiction, it goes beyond. In other words, we, the readers, are really free to find the same and exact kind of complexities in a Balzac novel, or for that matter in a Hitchcock film. I think the parallels between Robbe-Grillet and Hitchcock are astonishing, but they are contained in a much more conventional, if not wholly conventional style, in Hitchcock, whereas in Robbe-Grillet they're out there so that you almost don't need to look for them. It's so easy to read if not interpret a Robbe-Grillet novel, precisely because he gives us all the ways of doing it.

Roch Smith: Isn't there an element of what Pierre talked about as "*Transformation*", as an education of we his viewers and readers, that allows us to use these new skills on maybe a traditional novelist like Balzac and so forth?

Pierre Van den Heuvel: Je crois que les écrits de Robbe-Grillet sur lui-même sont toujours quelque peu provocateur. Ils provoquent l'innocence des autres. Il a un besoin immense de la reaction du lecteur, n'est-ce pas? Mais il donne d'abord, lui, une interprétation, mais qui est tournée de quelle manière qu'elle est provoquante, et qu'elle provoque des réactions, même contraires, n'est-ce pas?

Anthony Fragola: I want to go back to what Roch was saying, because I think ultimately, with film anyway, all we can do is interpret. I mean even though there are possibilities for multiple endings, contradictory scripts etc., nevertheless, because of the limitations of the material - the limitation of film itself which is absolutely linear, causal, linked - there's only one end, and there's only one narrative. Our interpretation of that narrative may be multiple, but there is only one, and its already pre-determined by Robbe-Grillet. I think that what Robbe-Grillet does, is, in a sense, the forerunner of possibilities that are beginning to emerge with new technologies such as CD-Rom. Because with CD-Rom one puts into place those elements with which one can then be truly in interactive participation. Right now you can only be a very active viewer-spectator/critical receptacle. There's no way that you can manipulate these sequences and reconstruct them in any significant way, because when you think about film, it's actually cemented, one shot to another shot.

In the Temple of Dreams

Royal Brown: But if there was a possibility, I don't think that Robbe-Grillet would go for the CD-Rom thing himself.

Anthony Fragola: I'm going to ask him.

Royal Brown: He had the possibility of making a film called *Piège à Fourrure,* in which the reels were to have been projected in an aleatory order, according to the flip of a coin of the projectionist - or whoever, or maybe the audience. And there have been films that have been shown in which the audiences can push buttons on the arms of their chairs and get different reels shown at a different time, so that even if CD-Roms made it easier, these types of experiments have already been done. Robbe-Grillet refused to make *Piège à Fourrure*, saying "Je tiens à contrôler le hasard" [I am intent on controlling chance], and I really don't think he would go for this CD-Rom thing. I don't think he would want people to manipulate his texts that way.

Tony Fragola: But then isn't the suggestion of a truly interactive reader-spectator really kind of a myth?

Royal Brown: I don't think it's a myth. I think the interactive reader has the most fun with a text that doesn't invite interaction, that doesn't seem to invite interaction, like Balzac, whereas Robbe-Grillet is appearing to invite interaction, when in fact he is doing all the interaction for you. That is sort of where I agree with you, but I wouldn't agree with the idea that the interpretation is fixed for the film. I think the reading of the film is fixed, in other words, the film has this absolutely inflexible order. But we still have open interpretation in the narrative isn't fixed, but the *passive reading* - I think there's a better word for it...

Roch Smith: That notion is supported by the film *N. Took the Dice*, which is made up of shots which were not used and out-takes from *Eden and After*, in which the aleatory element is visually shown, but in a sense is effectively meaningless, because as Tony said it's cemented together.

Delegate: Do you really think that Robbe-Grillet is still doing something new? What is new about his autobiographies in the context of what he was doing with his novels? And what is new about *Un Bruit Qui Rend Fou* which is different from *L'Homme Qui Ment*? Is it more our role as critics to find new ways of reading him, or do you think he is actually changing?

Raylene Ramsay: I do think that there's clearly a reflection on autobiography - on the conventions of autobiography - and I would read the first two *Romanesques* as doing something very effective, in fact, in looking at how we tell the stories of our lives. There's a whole reflection on the self, on the presence of the self to self. But I would agree, I think that in *Le Miroir Qui Revient* there is this reflection, and in *Angélique, ou l'Enchantement* there's a deeper level at which he's looking at the relationship between his own fantasies and the thematics of his work, but by the time we get to *La Mort de Corinthe* I have the

In the Temple of Dreams

feeling that there's very little that's new. However, it's very much like the most recent film in that there are very powerful images. I have the feeling that Robbe-Grillet would like to situate us as readers very much at the level of spotting the intertexts, spotting the references that we've met before. But there is a power to those images that I think is very distinctive, unique to Robbe-Grillet, I don't think we can deny it.

Ben Stoltzfus: Also, it is the return of the author, the revenge of the author, one might say, after the announcement that the author is dead! Suddenly we have the injection of the author's life in a fictional setting, and therefore earlier speakers talk of the "blurring of boundaries between the text and the writer", and indeed Robbe-Grillet is facing those boundaries and inviting his readers to view both as a kind of fictional language and therefore emphasizing the language of discourse which is a very important dimension of everything he is doing.

Roch Smith: It's interesting the way Raylene talked about *La Mort de Corinthe*, which was indeed Robbe-Grillet's original title, but he ended up calling it, for reasons you might want to imagine, *Les Derniers Jours de Corinthe*, which gives him a little more time perhaps.

Tony Fragola: Going back to your question related to film. I think he's beginning to do something that's very different in *Un Bruit Qui Rend Fou* that isn't fully explored. I think that we have possibilities of competing narratives in *Un Bruit Qui Rend Fou* that don't really materialize. I mean, you have one from Sarah la Blonde, you have one from the purported father, who comes into the story very late, whereas in his other films always one character - for example, either Boris in *L'Homme Qui Ment,* or Catherine in *L'Eden et Après* - begins to dominate the narrative. Or in *Glissements Progressifs du Plaisir* you have one person who dominates it, and people sort of work against that figure in the narrative. Here he uses a couple of more narratives that become much more open-ended, but they sort of die off, and I think that he's exploring something new in this piece, and I think that's one of the problems with the reception of that element of the piece. But I think structurally its very, very intersting too.

Royal Brown: I wouldn't even go that far. I think that one thing that's new about *Un Bruit Qui Rend Fou* is that it's almost a conventional film. It is certainly greatly lacking in the original editing style that marks Robbe-Grillet's best films. There is one interminable section of conversation between the police inspector and Nord, in which there is hardly any cutting at all, and what cutting there is, is totally conventional. I don't think the film works. I think it's a step back toward conventional film-making - perhaps because he worked with a collaborator, perhaps not, it's hard to say. I think that perhaps to a certain degree with *Le Miroir Qui Revient* Robbe-Grillet passes from the modern to the post-modern, that he's starting to break down the barriers of the various forms of fiction and he distinguishes between documentary and non-

In the Temple of Dreams

documentary. There's a film that is a follow up of the Ken Russell film *Whore*, called *Whore 2*, which is actually quite a brilliant piece of film-making, in which there is quite a bit of documentary footage, but for the two prostitutes that were killed, he has their stories re-enacted by actresses and so forth, or a film like *Paris is Burning*. There's a lot of breaking down of the barriers between fiction and non-fiction, between fiction and story-telling, and I think Robbe-Grillet's *Romanesques* is sort of fictional auto-biography that falls into that type of category. It's new for him. He was sort of the first author who was doing a lot of the things he did back when the *Nouveau Roman* kicked off. I think at this point he's more falling in step with a lot of other people, which is not necessarily bad. I liked *Le Miroir Qui Revient* a great deal. I do not like *Un Bruit Qui Rend Fou* at all, despite the striking images, for a lot of the images are striking. The film doesn't work: (a) as a Robbe-Grillet film, and (b) it doesn't work for me at all.

Ben Stoltzfus: Also that's related to the *Roland Barthes by Roland Barthes*, who has photographs of his early life and his family, and his mother, and his antecedents, with no captions whatsoever, and then he goes on to these fragments of discourse which are supposed to be his real autobiography; and therefore this is an intellectual autobiography rather than a conventional one, and therefore a reversal of the expectations that we regardless bring to the reading of these kinds of texts.

Ann Jefferson: Given what Robbe-Grillet said this morning about his anxiety about being classified - he was annoyed to have been classified as a novelist, as that made his role as a cinéaste problematic - and given I think what came out very clearly in the talk this morning about the parallels between the structure of the film and the autobiography, I wonder if one way in which Robbe-Grillet could be seen to be being new, is to be constantly offering new frames through which to assess something which perhaps hasn't changed: so there's a novelist Robbe-Grillet, a *Nouveau Roman* serialist Robbe-Grillet, a film Robbe-Grillet, and an autobiographer Robbe-Grillet, and I think that the thing about *Les Derniers Jours de Corinthe* is that there's a publisher Robbe-Grillet. He writes about contemporary literature in terms of a generation of writers which he presents himself as having helped to create and encourage. And I wonder what you think about the idea of these frames for assessment being constantly introduced by Robbe-Grillet; so he's suggesting all the time that we've been looking at him through the wrong frame, and there's a new one which invites a total reassessment, which disables us and leaves him in charge . . .

Royal Brown: *"Glissements Progressifs de Robbe-Grillet"?*

Ann Jefferson: Exactly!

Ben Stoltzfus: Yes, in addition to the frames you suggest there is also Robbe-Grillet the collaborator with David Hamilton, with Irina Ionesco, with

In the Temple of Dreams

Magritte, with Delvaux, and all of these dimensions which are certainly innovative and unusual, some more successful than others.

Roch Smith: And unfortunately poorly known, because it's difficult to get these books, except for *La Belle Captive*, which has been newly edited by Ben.

Delegate: Is it then with autobiography that Robbe-Grillet is doing something new in the present context?

Royal Brown: I think Robbe-Grillet definitely likes to avoid being pinned down. There's almost a phobic fear of being pinned down, raped, castrated, what have you, played out this way. He also is sort of his own "*man who lies*". A story that Robbe-Grillet tells is that Antonioni had in fact planned an ending for *Blow-Up*, and that he ran out of money, being sure the producer would not leave the film ambiguous like that, and he lost his bet, and his film had to come out without an explanation. The story has no basis in fact whatsoever, although Robbe-Grillet tells it quite often. Even in instances like that I think that he likes to play his own fool in the sense of the jester of *The Man Who Lies*. He likes to play his own characters and is constantly "*glisse*"-ing from one point to the other to avoid capture, as happens to Elias toward the end of *Trans-Europ-Express*.

Tony Fragola: It seems to me that with *La Belle Captive* the use of the images and text is something new.

Ben Stoltzfus: Yes it is, very much. And that's one of the reasons that he tried to do it the way he did it - his texts opposing Magritte's pictures, and Magritte's pictures contradicting the written text, and the reader being invited to collaborate in the production of meaning rather than the passive consumption of meaning. And so this is a very elaborate ritual that we are participating in, in order to come up with meaning. Otherwise there is no meaning, and you just sort of fall into the black hole and are left with nothing, and that's part of the creative process I believe.

Tony Fragola: I can't explain it on the spur of the moment, but it seems to me that *La Belle Captive* is a text which is much more open-ended than any of his films, especially *Un Bruit Qui Rend Fou*.

Ben Stoltztus: Yes, that's my feeling too, that it's one of the best open-ended texts, and Pierre could also comment on that, I'm sure.

Pierre Van den Heuvel: C'est difficile à dire. Le problème avec *La Belle Captive*, du côté du texte, c'est que les textes de *La Belle Captive* - des paragraphes, des pages entières, chapitres, figures en quatre livres différents - c'est la période, les années quatres-vingts, que Robbe-Grillet est arrivé, à mon avis, sur une piste close. Il a essayé, parce que c'est un expérimentateur, c'est pour ça qu'il essaie sur tous les moyens de briser ce que j'appelle en général des codes - les stéréotypes, les lieux communs etc. - comme les surréalistes. Alors il a commencé a expérimenter dans de différents genres, le roman, le

In the Temple of Dreams

film etc. ., où il a passé les mêmes textes. Et ça c'est une fois dangereuse, évidemment n'a pas donné grande chose, sauf cette combinaison admirable d'images et des mots dans *La Belle Captive*, n'est-ce pas? Donc, dans le livre. Et, du point de vue du film *La Belle Captive,* ça c'est tout à fait autre chose. Il y a un problème général sur Robbe-Grillet pour moi: c'est d'un côté qu'il veut nous imposer ces fabrications avec une lucidité extraordinaire. Ses oeuvres sont très ouvertes dans le sens ou l'écriture est l'avancement des mots et de la syntaxe, n'est-ce pas, la formation de l'histoire est présenté comme une montre ou un téléphone en plastique transforme. On voit les procédures, on voit les procédés de fabrication qu'on voit à travers - et là c'est très paradoxale. D'autre part, il proclame la primordialité du rêve, de l'imaginaire. C'est de la lucidité avec la méfiance du réel, et en même temps ces proclamations de la prédominance de l'imaginaire dans la vie même. Ça ira pas ensemble. C'est combiner l'ordinateur avec l'imaginaire. Ça, c'est un problème. Je ne sais pas ce que vous en pensez, si vous centrez sur là - également, dans les films où il donne des clins d'oeils, où il montre le trucage qu'il introduit lui-même.

Ben Stoltzfus: Despite the impasses, the personal impasses that you describe, I still think that *La Belle Captive* the novel remains a very enchanting and very open text in which the surrealism of Magritte and the textual experimentation of Robbe-Grillet come together in a very happy encounter, a fortuitous encounter, like the descending table that

Lautréamont describes. And therefore it's strange, and very interesting I find, that the surrealists of the 1920's - although Magritte practised his surrealism far beyond the 1920's of course - and the *Nouveau Roman,* should have come together in this remarkable way to produce this unusual text.

Royal Brown: I'd like to ask Ben a question about Magritte. A painter-friend of mine once said that he thought Magritte was a very bad painter, in other words, he was attacking Magritte as an artist, not for what he could obviously get out of his paintings, but for the technique and so forth. Do you think that this is true, and do you think that Robbe-Grillet is a better technician than Magritte? - though I sense that Magritte's technique certainly seems to go perfectly with what he's doing.

Ben Stoltzfus: That's an interesting question. In a sense he is a bad painter, because if he were painting realistic paintings, no-one would take him seriously. If he were trying to paint holes in the walls that are realistic paintings, he would be dismissed - every painting of his would be in the dustbin, I suspect. But his extraordinary imagination lifts them up beyond the ordinary, and there maybe the technique is part of the bourgeois mentality that he so acidly criticizes, that is, part of his technique is to be bad!

Judith Stoltzfus: I'd just like to add to that also that he paints that way on purpose. As an illustrator it's part of his language, to say what he's saying the way that he says it.

In the Temple of Dreams

Ian Christie: I think there's a parallel there. The other great surrealist painter who is clearly judged by some to be a bad painter is Dali, of course, and much obloquy denies him as a painter, because he doesn't fit into the role of ordinism in painting. But I think there are other points of view possible, although whether those points of view demand that you step inside a particular surrealist aesthetic is an interesting question - very similar to the debate just after the release of *Last Year at Marienbad,* that contrasted Resnais, as a *real filmmaker*, showing what could be done with his material, as compared with Robbe-Grillet, as an *amateur film-maker*, a bad film-maker, trying to animate his own material. Now I think that increasingly doesn't look like a sensible basis for comparison, means to comparison. But it's kind of that again that the reception of the new film, since it was first seen in Berlin, has re-evoked. The same desire to separate the material from the method of treatment, which is precisely what Robbe-Grillet is actually working on. He's working on that interface between the notion of material and method of treatment, and the work constantly throws back a kind of critical response which falls into the trap, one of the many traps that he sets I think, just as the viewer of Magritte falls into many traps.

Tony Fragola: Well, do you know, the same criticism was heaped on Bunuel. But if you look at a film like *Viridiana*, the technique in *Viridiana* is great, but it's seamless, and it's invisible in a sense. Basically, they are true surrealists. Because the surrealists didn't give a damn, supposedly, about technique. "If I am anti-Art, why should I be artistically perfect?" If you fall into the bourgeois trap that they are attacking, you then start playing their own game - so he takes a whole different technique. And the whole idea of slicing the eye is not only to shock but also to prepare the viewer to see reality in a new way, and to cut off all that bourgeois art up to that point, so that I don't think you can use the same criteria for judgement.

Royal Brown: I would agree. I wish I'd had the weapons to answer the questions back then, which I didn't, and which was a long time ago.

Ben Stoltzfus: I'd like to ask Raylene to elaborate a little bit on a statement that suggested men prefer women who flit back and forth between the submissive role and the inventive-aggressive role, and I just wondered if you would comment a little further on the sources of your information.

Raylene Ramsay: I think that was in the context of an interview by Christine D. in 1995, in France, talking about the sado-masochistic environment, its practices, its community, and one of the comments that she did make was that. But these rituals are really very finite, and are limited in number. Catherine Robbe-Grillet has written a classic novel, *The Dominatrix*, and another book called *Image*, in the latter of which she situates herself very much at the feminine-masochistic pole, while in *Cérémonie des Femmes* she situates herself as a dominatrix at the opposite pole - not passive, but very reactive -

In the Temple of Dreams

the pole of masculinity if you like. But when Christine D. discusses these rituals, she says they almost always include scenarios played out by women with other women, so that women become bisexual - one plays the role of the voyeur in a very voyeuristic scenario. So I guess I was trying to suggest that there were some parallels between the thematics and the rituals that exist in a sadomasochistic universe, and those that Robbe-Grillet transposes in very lurid fashion into his texts, which he called "*the impoverished rituals of the sadomasochistic confrérie*". Clearly, this is a world he knows, and that he has a relationship with, but I do think that these rituals inform his own texts in quite obvious ways. Christine D. suggests that men in a sadomasochistic universe don't - are unable to - situate themselves at both the feminine or the masculine pole, that they can't play these games. I would suggest that in Robbe-Grillet's texts - and this is very much my thesis - Robbe-Grillet *as narrator* tends always to situate himself at the pole of control, the masculine pole, the pole that I would call the sadistic, as opposed to the masochistic. So I guess that's what I'm trying to say.

Royal Brown: I think that starts to emerge a bit in his last films. As long as you have Trintignant in his films, even though he plays to some extent the fool, it's still really a positive character. By the time you get to the really absurd Philippe Noiret character in *Playing with Fire*, and then the Walter Mesguich character in *The Beautifiul Captive* - and again he's a total wimp - and then the character in *The Blue Villa*, who again

I have a great deal of difficulty relating to in any way, shape or form, he, [like the others] seems like such a total non-entity, almost as if his [ARG's] films consciously or unconsciously are showing the breakdown of his sense of self. I mentioned to him that I really didn't like his actor who played the Nord character in *The Blue Villa*, and he said "Oh, I love his acting. I think he's a great actor", and so I sort of backed off. In the last three films there does seem to be a move away from this, into not so much taking on the passive role that he would attribute to women - which is purely a gender issue and not a sex issue - but into a period of decline where he simply can't keep the control going any more, and there's to me a very strong sense of *woman*; the Philippe Noiret character in *Playing with Fire* is a completely ineffectual human being, and pretty much the same can be said of the character in *The Beautiful Captive* as well. And I just wonder whether there isn't this sort of sense of a breakdown of a sense of self.

Raylene Ramsay: I think I would agree although I would also like to say that the characters are not the narrator, and the narrator is not single, having all those different levels operating. I think very often "male" characters are situated at the feminine pole, and the "female" at the pole of the masculine, for example the magistrate in *Progressive Slidings towards Pleasure*. But my sense is that Robbe-Grillet himself sets forth from the pole of control, the narrative control, the characters. But yes, there is an experimentation if you like but I just don't feel that there's a breakdown that is binary concerning masculine/feminine, whereas there is a breakdown in a number of binary systems, and I think that that is part of the power of his work.

Roch Smith: I'd like to go back to a question that was asked earlier about what is new in Robbe-Grillet. One area in which I don't think much has been done, has to do with the relationship of Robbe-Grillet and music, and it's very striking in *The Blue Villa*, where Wagner is used with a very renewing effect. The same can be found, to a lesser degree, with the film *The Beautiful Captive*, with the use of Schubert's and Wagner's music again. Robbe-Grillet is very interested in Wagner, and I don't know of anybody who's actually explored that very far. That may yield a lot, but no-one's really considered it seriously yet. There may even be some ways in which the Wagnerian stories relate to the novels themselves. One of the things that happens as you look at the later works of Robbe-Grillet, whether the novels or films, is that it gives you a fresh perspective each time. I think all of us experience that. While I had classified, pigeon-holed, the *Dutchman* in *Eden and After* as *Duchamp*, he's also the *Flying Dutchman*, and he is the stranger. There's much to be said about the arrival of the stranger, the disruptive arrival of a stranger in Robbe-Grillet, for example. These are things that become to me more apparent as I see later works and use these as a filter to look back.

Royal Brown: Well, Ross says that Wagner is the first person to structurally study myths, therefore in other words the whole convention of the '*leitmotif*' device and so forth he's actually giving a structural explication of the myths that he's studying in the musical structure.

Raylene Ramsay: Robbe-Grillet does talk about the pleasures and dangers of Wagner's music. He sees it as something which could swallow him up, identifies it with the sea. So there is a femininity if you like, to Wagner's music.

Roch Smith: And there's a masculinity to Wagner's music that is threatening as well.

Royal Brown: Referring to *La Belle Captive*, one reason that Michel Fano didn't work on the film, was that he refused to play around with Wagner's music. You can play around with Verdi, yet you can't play around with Wagner, and so what Robbe-Grillet did was to use the opening of *Das Rheingold* slowed down to half its speed, which Fano had to deal with, and that is a sort of defence against having to evolve any music.

Roch Smith: As viewers of *The Blue Villa* will note, there's an interesting connection with another Wagnerian opera, *Tristan and Isolde*, which is also of course French. And the ending of the film is much more to do with this French legend than with *The Flying Dutchman*.

Ben Stoltzfus: Certainly music is another frame, and Robbe-Grillet's collaboration with Michel Fano and the use of soundtrack is part of the innovative dimension that fits into the other collaboration [end].

00. Alain Robbe-Grillet

Bibliography

[*List of Robbe-Grillet's publications, September 1996*]

Un Régicide (1949) - Novel [only published in 1978]
[A Regicide]

Les Gommes (1951) - Novel (*Prix Fénéon, 1954*)
[The Erasers]

Le Voyeur (1955) - Novel (*Prix des Critiques, 1955*)
[The Voyeur]

La Jalousie (1957) - Novel
[Jealousy]

Dans le Labyrinthe (1959) - Novel
[In the Labyrinth]

Instantanés (1954-1962) - Short Stories
[Snapshots]

Pour un Nouveau Roman (1953-1963) - Essays
[For a New Novel]

La Maison de Rendez-Vous (1965) - Novel
[The "Maison de Rendez-Vous"]

Projet pour une Révolution à New York (1970)
[Project for a Revolution in New York] - Novel

Reves de Jeunes Filles (1971) - with David Hamilton
[Dreams of Young Girls]

**Construction d'un Temple en Ruines
à la Déesse Vanadé** (1975) - with Paul Delvaux
[Construction of a Temple in Ruins
to the Goddess Vanadé]

La Belle Captive (1976) - with René Magritte
[The Beautiful Captive]

Topologie d'une Cité Fantôme (1976) - Novel
[Topology of a Phantom City]

Souvenirs du Triangle d'Or (1978) - Novel
[Recollections of the Golden Triangle]

Traces Suspectes en Surfaces (1972-1978) - with
[Suspect Traces on Surfaces] /Robert Rauschenberg

Temple aux Miroirs (1979) - with Irina Ionesco
[Temple of Mirrors]

Le Rendez- Vous (1981) - Textbook
[The Meeting]

Djinn. Un Trou Rouge entre les Pavés Disjoints
[Djinn. A Red Crevice between Broken Pavestones]
- Novel (1981, Same text as *Le Rendez-Vous*)

Le Miroir Qui Revient (1984) - Autobiography
[Ghosts in the Mirror]

Angélique, ou l'Enchantement (1987)
[Angélique, or Enchantment] - Autobiography

Les Derniers Jours de Corinthe (1993)
[The Last Days of Corinth] - Autobiography

Filmography

[*List of Robbe-Grillet's feature films, September 1996*]

L'Année Dernière à Marienbad (1961) - Screenplay
[Last Year at Marienbad] - (*First Prize at Venice 1961/ Méliès Award - Best Picture of the Year/André Bazin Gold Medal/Oscar Nom. for Best Screenplay 1962*)

L'Immortelle (1962) (*Prix Louis Delluc, 1963*)
[The Immortal One]

Trans-Europ-Express (1966)
[Trans-Europ-Express]

L'Homme Qui Ment (1968)
[The Man Who Lies] (*Berlin, Best Screenplay, 1968*)

L'Eden et Après (1971)
[Eden and After]

N.a Pris les Dés (1971) - Film for Television
[N. Took the Dice]

Glissements Progressifs du Plaisir (1974)
[Progressive Slidings towards Pleasure]

Le Jeu avec le Feu (1975)
[Playing with Fire]

La Belle Captive (1983)
[The Beautiful Captive]

Taxandria (1989) - Story only

Un Bruit Qui Rend Fou (1995)
[The Blue Villa] (*San Diego, Best Film, 1996*)

"Or, je ne suis pas un romancier. Je suis ingénieur de recherches agronomiques, spécialiste des maladies de bananes. Alors, tous vont me demander - *comment est-ce qu'un ingénieur de recherches agronomiques peut écrire des romans?*"

Printed in Great Britain
by Amazon

79417480R10098